SLAVE MOTH

SLAVE MOTH

A Narrative in Verse

THYLIAS MOSS

A Karen & Michael Braziller Book

PERSEA BOOKS / NEW YORK

Persea Books, Inc.
853 Broadway
New York, NY 10003

Library of Congress Cataloging-in-Publication Data
Moss, Thylias.
Slave moth : a narrative in verse / by Thylias Moss.
p. cm.
"A Karen & Michael Braziller book."
ISBN 0-89255-289-1 (alk. paper)
1. African American women—Poetry. 2. Women slaves—Poetry.
3. Tennessee—Poetry. 4. Liberty—Poetry. 5. Slavery—Poetry. I. Title.

PS3563.O8856S55 2003
811'.54—dc21   2003003624

Designed by Rita Lascaro

Typeset in Aldus

Printed in the United States in America

First Edition

CONTENTS

SLAVE MOTH

DELICACIES

My master is a collector.
Rare things delight him.
Deformity piques in him an unwholesome joy
that encourages repeated fellowship
with curiosity

that will not cease
until he himself has milked every animal with more than
or less than the right number of anything,
roasting their hearts and livers for himself only,
making himself sicker with delicacy
and only delicacy
to which he has a devotion.

He has called it *succulence*

which he was tempted to call me
when my birth caused the death of his horse, *Varl,*
the succulence of that power, snakebite and misery,
Kentucky racehorse dropping dead by the fence
at the precise moment of my first cry
in my first darkness outside Mamalee,
Varl whose name became mine though not enough
(maybe none at all) of her tamed spirit
—so I, Varl Perry, delight him even more.

Peter Thomas Perry might prefer if it were me
outlined in anatomical charts made by his hand
of one-good-eye and three-legged pigs
he got cheap at auction in Chattanooga
when the last of the Cherokee were leaving
though he would have sold his soul.
The smokehouse was already crowded

with ham and sausage
when he succumbed to his science.
His private bacon, renderings; private
batch of soap made for him from deformed hog fat
by his slave Albino Pearl
also acquired at auction, *White
African* she's called when Peter Perry
wants quick money from lookers
quick to pay it. I've seen it happen.

Something amazing is behind such things.
He loathes, fears, desires it.
Something tantalizing. Paralyzing.

He left his *Great Book of Insectean Marvels*
on his desk, opened to the page on *Actias luna*
moths flying at night like green angels of the insects,
and this morning as I cleaned the room
that is a torture chamber
for his illiterate wife Ralls Janet,
I read about how luna moths commit
all their energy to finding a mate
—they don't have much time, less than a week
for a life, soundless, they don't have mouths,
ears, don't have to eat, don't take any orders
except from their own nature
all under darkness.

What do they matter?

Pale green stars falling into my hands.
Obedient to luring odors.
The smell of something within themselves,
compelling scent connects them.

Master Perry wanted me to see that page,
expected my interest to pique upon my learning
how the luna larva makes itself a cocoon
of silky parts, papery parts
inside of which it writes itself a new existence
and changes to fit it; larva goes in,
Actias luna comes out.

Learning more and more
about how to be his slave—what can I do
with insectean information? What can I do
with it; how can it take on value
for a slave? How can it matter?
What circumstances can it change?

I'm a rare thing, and my reading amuses Master Perry,
the speed with which I reach out
and grab onto understanding.
I am just lucky, if a slave can have luck, that such
a man as Peter Perry demanded an experiment
with reading, curious about how well could a black girl
do it; I am his experiment, me benefiting
from great minds and arguments he was exposed to
in college out east near Chesapeake, interrupted
when he inherited this farm and had ideas

which still include Mamalee reading to him and reciting
to him in moonlight, talking books in the woods, classics,
Ralls Janet not close enough to make out words,
at the distance where it sounds like buzzing, rumors
of war. I can see what's happening to her.
There is deformity in this arrangement, too.

Can't do any of this in the open since Ralls Janet
came here as his bride nine years ago. She hated
what she took to be the ranking: Peter Perry, Mamalee,
me, Ralls Janet in the hierarchy of intelligence.
In her experience, what went on here, place Peter
Perry was calling Perrysburg, Tennessee, should mean
the punishment and death of us.
There were not many who would approve, especially
among Peter Perry's in-laws and relatives.
Especially Ralls Janet who couldn't appreciate
the oddity that her presence expanded.

My power over her
that I can read in her behavior.
I used to sleep right outside the master's bedroom
door, all his slaves in his house till she came
and ordered us into a cabin she persuaded
her husband to have his slaves build. The one
of her requests he honored.

It amuses Master Peter when his Ralls Janet
watches how little reading has done for me,
Varl, who for all her intelligence is just a slave.
Still a slave. No better off it would seem.
She saw me this morning, and as I left the room
I saw her tracing over the luna drawing with her finger
that wasn't quite as fat as the luna larva.

she's gotten quieter and quieter.
Unintentionally emphasized the larva
and did me a favor.

—You can fit all of my name *Varl* into larva.
You can fit all of my name into something
that undergoes complete metamorphosis.

Starting tonight

I won't write any more of my thoughts on paper
though I did like to steal it from the master,
Ralls Janet especially perturbed by that
to the amusement of her husband;
starting tonight

on cloth I stitch my words,
the larva drawing its silk back and forth
through squares of cloth

that will be luna wings, dozens
of specimens stitched together, connected
into a cocoon I can wear under my dress
these first squares pinned
across my chest to change my heart,
the next ones to be the underside
of my scarf those days I choose to
tie up my hair to change my mind
and then keep it from changing back.

Lunas don't give up their wings
and become caterpillars again
eating all the time, as insatiable
as Peter Perry.

All luna underneath
the visible Varl

so that anybody who sees me, even Master Perry
who lately looks at me too long, investing me
with his evening, so that he's in the mental picture
he carries of me bending over his book, finding my destiny
in his book left for me to find it, Peter Perry,
master of my destiny. He can hold onto me
in the worst ways.

THE JIMBO WOOD

When under my dress I'm wearing my cocoon,
I like to smooth my dress in the presence
of Ralls Janet
as if I'm spreading my words.

I stitch a little moth in one of the corners
of each cloth page, affirming the possibilities
of my identity. Helps me stay who I am
to do this.

The pages button one to another
so I can move them around
make a puzzle of my experience.
Read this page first or this one,
get a new meaning of what happened
and what I felt depending
on the sequence. A buttoning quilt
of a cocoon whose purpose is for changing.

Steal buttons from Ralls Janet's dresses,
from skirts, shirts; one at a time, from this sleeve,
next time another; my favorite buttons
that I sewed on just to take them back.
She thinks I deliberately sabotage her dresses
as only hers lose buttons rapidly. I told her
birds and squirrels think they're seeds and nuts
and take them while her dresses hang outside
drying and tempting.
"They look just like the heart of a peapod,
those green glass ones that close-match your eyes,"
but really match much better the wings
of a luna.

She can't believe it, so many skills
in just one pretty (she thinks it) little slavegirl:
reader, scholar, seamstress, laundress, nurse
(if I have to), temptress, gardener, cook, weaver
—as if I'd been to every school, now the one
in her home studying science
of deception and disrespect. Excelling.

I prefer to do my stitch-writing on this tree stump
where by writing I'm also making a reflection of myself
that an ordinary mirror can't produce.
Ralls Janet watches me over her shoulder
from a mirror while I'm sewing for her,
putting characteristic *varls*
which are tiny knotted stitches
in the seams and also putting my initials, *VP*
on everything I make that she and her daughter wear.

After sundown, dark settled in, slave work done
I write through to past midnight, Dob bringing me
a little something to eat that's warm.
His warm company, too. Though I am not opposed
to snacking on fresh insects
if it means I get to write more. One once
tasted somewhat of cloves.
I show him when I stitch
his warm company, too.
He likes that. And soon, he'll be liking me.
More. Kindness breeds more kindness; makes you
deserving.

This tree stump has become a father to me.
I call him the Jimbo Wood. I had to name him.
Before I stitch a word I run my hand across
remarkable muscles hard and durable as iron.
An indestructible father.
I had to name him for his kindness.

The Jimbo Wood is an anchor for me.
When I sit here, write here, dream of my Dob here,
sit with my Dob here (he will be mine), it's like I'm
on the deck of one of the ships my father's leased to.
But what must it really be like standing on a ship
like the ones that carry Africans to this despair?
What goes through his mind? Named *Odysseus*
calling himself *Captain*. Could he become a murderer?
How important is revenge? What are the limits?
The Roupers (Peter Perry's relative owners of the shipyards)
are as good as the circumstances will allow.
—But what made those circumstances? What made those
deformed pigs? What made Peter Perry love them
alive, then dissect and devour them, and love that taste better?

I'm sewing muscle into my cocoon,
powerful muscles of my thoughts

and I'm going to ask my Dob (he will be mine)
to make me a box from this stump,
if he can get enough wood off it,
where I will keep my cocoon pages
when I need to take them off,
Ralls Janet threatening to burn them or something
if she knew about and could find them. She keeps away
from Jimbo's powers.

Wide stump. Peter Perry's slaves
all five of us
can sit around it like a table.
Polished darkening surface
good for lessons spelled out
in beans or corn makes it
look just like a stringent rationing
of food is the reason we have gathered.
I do that when Jessper Staley

comes over, but she scoops up the beans
and puts them in a pocket. Scared
of how she'd act with too much knowledge.
Scared of my example.
I install plenty
of deep, deep pockets.

Wood from this tree was made into a fine oak bed
for the master's new wife, which was Ralls Janet.
Captain (my father) and Dwarf Sully chopped it down.
My father who builds ships as well as sails on them
was the one who made the bed. Some
of his spit and blood deepened the color of the wood
it seeped into. He makes coffins, too.
So did my dead brothers.
So does Dwarf Sully. My Dob can, too.
(He will be mine)

After Captain (my father—I'm proud of that name)
finished the bed, he was hired out to Baltimore
to work for Peter Thomas Perry's Aunt Baly-Belinda
who raised Peter when he was orphaned, sent him
to school, who still sends him a modest stipend,
who married a Rouper about thirty years ago,
a Rouper who was son of a woman who was an Adler
before she married, but the Roupers did quite well
on their own, buying up some factories and shipyards
all along the Atlantic, north and south. Few companies
could manage without the Roupers as their agents.
Adler whiskey and Heffring (it's Ralls Janet *Heffring* Perry)
cider travel well.

Baly-Belinda took on some agency herself
and was as good at that as her husband.
They paid a black man, red man, any man good wages

if not the same wages. It was the work that mattered.
We're all brown here, her husband once said, working
in the sun.

When Mr. Rouper died in an accident at his dry dock
Baly-Belinda dressed up in his clothes and conducted all
the business as her own shaven son just through
with college, Baly Rouper. She became known
for her navigation. She was dressed as a woman
when she got off the ship in Europe, or came to Perrysburg
to visit her nephew and smoke tobacco, but not
when she went to church.

When she wrote to Master Peter, which was not often,
she enclosed a note for me informing me of her progress,
which was not much, in trying to locate Captain Perry.

For her nephew, some of it to be shared with Mamalee
or Ralls Janet at his discretion, which was predictable,
foreign coins, strange spice leaves almost powder
when they got here, odd dead butterflies and even odder
things with wings.

Master Peter suggested strongly that Captain likely killed
Mr. Rouper, so Master Peter figured on collecting
a hefty bounty for turning Captain in. His strange hair
as coppery as his guilt.

Aunt B-B's P.S. : Don't worry; I'll never find him.

Since then Captain hasn't come back.
Since then I've believed him free somewhere
(except of his guilts and regrets)
counting on me and Mamalee, his family,
to free ourselves and join him
in a life worth imagining.

Since then, Captain hasn't been in Peter Perry's way.
Since then I've been coming to Jimbo Wood.

Does Captain still think of Mamalee as wife?
Does Mamalee still think of Captain as husband?
If not, what are they to each other?

Peter Perry is still Ralls Janet's husband.
Ralls Janet is still Peter Thomas Perry's wife.

Ralls Janet is afraid of Jimbo wood
She doesn't like for her darling little Lusa
to sit on this stump,
to sit in this old man's lap, sharp, and welcoming
to bugs and animal musks. Afraid of a splinter
in her daughter's darling little rump. Afraid
of almost everything.
A honeybee. A moth. I sit here
as much as I can. Peter Perry knows it.
I wonder how Ralls Janet manages to sleep
in her Captain-built and poisoned bed?

With the roots and all, the stump
looks like an enormous spider.

My father once got a letter to us through traveling men
who do some circulation business with Aunt B-B
and Mamalee, and let us know he'd been to England and Japan,
but it's been a long time since we've heard from him
and I can't picture him as well as I used to
and he's no longer part of what I have to deal with.
Maybe he'll write a book and publish it in London.
His adventures.

That he's gone isn't strange.
Jessper doesn't even know her father
and she was sold away from her mother to the Staleys
who didn't want to buy (*Theodore* Staley didn't)
her very productive mother
who could do the work of three, four, then five,
one more every time Jessper tells it, stubborn mules.
And every time, I tell Jessper that I am even
more impressed. Into the sad hundreds.

And who was Dob's father? Dob's mother?
I've never heard him say. Never heard him wonder.

I visit Jessper at the Staleys at night
and on Sundays when I'm not writing, not enough
I know, Jessper by herself there, the only slave there
through the night, but I haven't been with her
when a stray something wanders into the room.
"It won't come if you're here, Varl."
I'm no adequate protection; how can she say to me
what she doesn't believe? What will not be put in writing?
I'm no more than her, just like her in the barn, no threat
against what's coming
and that's why I slip back here, clear of Staley
property. Coward Varl. Sensible Varl. Regretful.
Is it wrong to put this writing first? Myself?
How to think straight when everything's so twisted?

Jessper doesn't get to say much there.
No Staley talks much.
Very respectful of the tongue; if it lies
still, it can't get bitten by your teeth.
They're not religious.

What can I do for Jessper but encourage her to run?
I can't run away for her, and I don't have to go yet;
no immediacy of physical assault, some joy in rankling
Ralls Janet, diverting and claiming her husband's attention
though I do not really want it. Besides,
it's not that easy, so far to freedom, desperate men
to bring you back in any condition for dollars.
Jessper's so suspicious she'd let no one help her. A few blacks
turning in runaways in exchange for their master's promise
of manumission and some money to get started. A few.
A few black masters, too. They interest Peter Perry.
He's known a few.

I lean over and kiss Jimbo Wood goodnight.

DUBE STYLE

It must seem ridiculous,
the result
of some extremely deformed thinking
that reading and writing slaves, me and Mamalee,
don't run away, as we could so easily,

maybe I'm just a page in the master's book;
free in my thoughts, but attached to the binding.
I can turn but not exit—how ridiculous;

I'm flesh, blood, thought, feeling; not paper.
It should be so easy.

For instance:
soon as the ink's dry on the papers of permission
Mamalee writes out to see a sick mother in Virginia
and work tobacco for her mama's master;
and the papers are tucked
into her borrowed morning coat

along with papers of permission to see
a master black stonecutter up Chesapeake way
for a marker for Mamalee's mama's grave
in case her death really does come
as soon as we think it will, though we hope
it doesn't, preferring a reprieve

for Mamalee's mama who, in this telling,
was the mistress of the plantation since
it had to have one and the master of Litchfield,
an only child, did not ever marry; soon as the ink's dry,
we leave

—If not by train then by foot
hiding in the open, soot on our faces and arms
in streaks like the patterns on bark,
our clothes crumpled the same
so we blend into sycamore and cottonwood
we wrap ourselves around

all the way to the Ohio River
and a flat boat for the crossing
that disrupts the star mirror
that the river is,

slicing holes,
cutting disappearance
into the sky's reflection.

A patch, a square
big as a quilt
of stars
goes out.

Our teabark faces don't pick up
the reflection of any stars,
just our eyes, dark part
of our eyes fill with constellations.

It could be like that so easily.

But instead, we stay put in the clearer-cut bondage
of the south and not in the north's rather deceptive
manumission where what's really felt about you
might not ever be known; my freedom won't make
anybody care about me. That's the point I figure;
anybody is free not to care. And any white body
in the south is free not to have slaves. There's a few

who appreciate their freedom.
Some because they're poor.

Mamalee's got her claim
to this land, good land
that every lick of the hoe
writes her name on

to be Leticia Lee's property
not Peter Thomas Perry's.

If you get up there high enough, high
as the roof, if you hang on
to a bird, bat, luna moth, climb in
a hot-air balloon like what Peter Perry craves
(would you be free up there, free in the air
above Tennessee? Or property there, too?),
you see how Mamalee through the years
has shaped the rows of corn
to grow into the letters of her name,
a deed spelled out. Entitlement.

It's hers.

And not even slavery can make her deny it.
Beautiful land. All those pine trees on the chain
of hills, all that jewelry. Frogs filling
the roads and singing to her

but I don't feel the bond that she feels.
Her bond's sincere, not experimental.

The land shaped her, too.

When Master Peter acquired Mamalee, she was already
reading and writing according to the orders
of her previous mistress, who was Esmenda Jenkins Dube
the first, because Esmenda Jenkins Dube the first
didn't want any stupidity around her; she couldn't
stand it. Stupidity gave her headaches

so she started teaching her slaves to read
so nobody could deceive them,
so she could just write out her orders
and distribute them
to her reading and writing
uppity educated household.
Fancy hand-styled manuals called
The Dube Style and Rule Book.

When she passed them out, she told her pupils
that she knew the ability to read
would make running away even more tempting,
but they could read for themselves how
dangerous it would be traveling so far
with nothing

but the attitude reading and writing
gives you.

If they got caught by someone without
her way of thinking
which was the threat of much of the south
they'd likely be killed they'd been so ruined
—to the point they'd be much better at being masters
than being slaves. So ruined. But if they stayed,

her house would be their inheritance,
so she instructed them to use the logic she was also
instructing them in; *think* she said, she was old then

and wasn't immortal, she would die
before they knew it
and didn't need the help of any of them
because she knew the way there by herself.
Then they would have something.
First word they learned was m-a-n-u-m-i-s-s-i-o-n.

But mostly, they would have the house
of their memories.

The house that was really more theirs than hers
because the amount of living they did there
all added up. The cumulative living.

Only five of them, so house enough
for all of them, considering that including her
it had been six. They wouldn't have to kill
each other off. Or one could buy
the others' shares, allowing them
reasonable profit. That would be fair.

She'd loved a black man. She'd married a white man.

Esmenda Jenkins Dube the first was all about fair
and saw her house as an oasis in the middle
of corruption, saw herself as a missionary
converting stupidity into reason. She thought
that was much more useful than a miracle.

Mamalee, the best reader, *brilliant,* Esmenda said
soon got to teach.
Esmenda and Leticia each led a class.
Teaching slaves to read and write and furthering
her own skills, dusting Esmenda's library, dusting
each page of all the books, some with gold crusted edges,
became the only work she did for Esmenda

who had Mamalee call her "Esmenda"
and whom called Mamalee "Leticia."
Refined school. Dube sympathizers
teaching arts and trades, taking on apprentices,
so slaves could earn money masters didn't know about.

"You're going to college," Esmenda eventually said
and Mamalee did, with Esmenda,
an old woman (marvelous actress playing herself
more feeble than she'd ever be) who needed assistance
from her personal slave in all her classes.
Mamalee was right beside her learning, too,
learning better and for free,
just as Esmenda had planned and suspected.

More like daughter and her white mother
who wasn't afraid to love a black man as
any good man or good woman should be loved.
Esmenda didn't feel threatened, but compensated
by Mamalee's existence .

She'd loved a black man but hadn't had a child.

The Dube Mercy School was established in the shed.
where slaves from other farms came to help the widow
who paid their masters just as if they had done
some planting, plowing, or harvesting instead of
going to school. They helped the school have necessity.

Pupils couldn't come often enough; crop work did
have to get done, for the pupils' masters and for
Esmenda. The widow couldn't live
just off inheritance
(not lavishly)
from the death of suspiciously wealthy Elston Jenkins
whose seamstresses sold dresses all around the world.

Special fermented cotton no one else could grow.
The exceptional silk of drunken silkworms.
It worked. Bribes, too.
(*Dube* was her name before she married and she liked it,
saw no reason to change it.)

Mamalee prayed for rain everyday, or drought,
long-lasting winter, so to shut down
work on the farms and claim the slaves' idle time
for day school beyond midnight school when some
could sneak away; never knew how many, or if any
could come, if that night an alphabet of shadows

would emerge from the trees and open the shared books,
and write on slates with chalks that seemed such
chunks of moon, the writers had to check to see
the whole moon still bright over shoulders.

But some slaves
grew jealous of E and L, the cozy between them,

some slaves from other farms
who had to do what they called *real work*
and became a threat to the secret
and thought they really wanted to read about
the demise of the one who was teaching them to read.
They learned to spell trouble on their own.

Men started coming, leaving papers around
with Negro insults all over them
to see would Leticia Lee react while she worked
in the room while they were there
going over their pretenses with Esmenda.
Mamalee just cleaned around the papers, didn't let
any glint of knowing form in her squirrel-colored eyes.
Eventually, one of the men stayed longer, mustached man

prone to good eating,
according to Mamalee's look at him in her recollections.
She took him for the devil's cousin, since
he didn't look as good as the devil
would be sure to look to tempt you better, so
at best, the devil's cousin.
"Miz Jenkins, I hear tell you got a school for Negroes
here—is that true, Miz Jenkins?"

He and most others would not acknowledge
Esmenda Dube's insistence on maintaining *Dube*
as she had done too long years ago at thirty-four
to stop maintaining it just because of marriage.
She told Mamalee that Elston Jenkins loved her too much
just the way she was (black lover and all)
to change anything about her, "change nothing,"
he once said in the craziness of courting
and she didn't.

"You ever live at a school, Ralph Littleton?
Or did you hurry away the moment school was over,
so fast you took all evidence of your having been there
with you? Is that where people want to live,
when they failed as many tests as you did?

This is my home.
I don't go to school anymore. Want to see
my certificates of completion? And seeing as
my last certificate was from a 'finishing school,'
you'd do best to consider me finished just
as the school did.
Instead, how about if Leticia here
gets you something?"

"No, thank you, unless she can get me a teacher.
You know anything about that, Gal?"

"No, Sir. I don't know much at all."

"Would you like to know something, Gal?
You would, wouldn't you?"

"No, Sir. I knows what I needs to know
to keep my mistress' fields producing.
If she don't eat
I don't eat either.
That's what I'm all of a fixed on."

"That sounds right, Miz Jenkins. Her ignorance
seems sincere, but we're watching now. I hope
it don't turn out for you that this is a smart one
up to trickery we just can't let loose in the county,
spreading it in plenty of *Nigra* younguns we also
don't want let loose. We have to think about
the safety of good people like you. You know
it's what your Elston would want. I'm just stepping
in for him like he would've done for my family
if something had of happened to me.
We look out for each other. You're lucky to live
in the south where we do that. Wouldn't want
education to give some Nigra ideas about
better wives, if you know what I mean.
You could be in danger. The word might get out
that this is one of those unwholesome stations
if I let it out by accident. We can't let loose
that *Nigra* trickery because
letting it loose would be like shooting ourselves
and turning our intelligence into ignorance.
It's not even supposed to be possible to turn intelligence
into ignorance. Naturally we're among the best in
everything we do, but not in the impossible, and we want
to keep the impossible, impossible. Then we got
harmony in the county, and harmony in the state.

Everybody likes harmony, Miz Jenkins. You and me
are in harmony right now; isn't this a right fine harmony?
I've never seen one better, and you haven't either.
But there's not any harmony if this *Nigra* gal is acting
like she can't read in order to bring forth *my* ignorance.
But that's not what she's doing, is it? So I'm going
to smile at what that gal said, *this* time."

Good thing he said he was smiling
because Mamalee told me you couldn't tell; nothing much
happened to his mouth. He showed the most teeth
when he said *gal.*

"I like you, Miz Jenkins, so let me put it another way.
Your late husband was without equal in these parts,
a great inventor; I made a fortune because of him,
and I know he wouldn't put up with this treason
of teaching slaves. I'm doing what he would've done,
perhaps not the same way he would have done it,
but I'm stopping you from ruining yourself
—and ruining the good name of this county
that we have earned beating back the abolitionists,
and maintaining our harmony.
I value my life and the good lives of my community
—which you used to belong to, but look here—"

He pulled out a map with the county lines redrawn.

"—look here at how you're not inside the circle;
look at how excluding you gave the county
a tighter circle—looks sacred now, don't it?
It moved a step above harmony to sacred.
I don't think much of anybody important will want
to give up this tight circle just to let you back in,
but I'll see what I can do for you
if you're going to behave. It don't look right

for a fine lady like yourself to be surrounded
by Nigras. You don't have any reputation left
when I say you don't. I like you, Miz Jenkins,
we all . . . *like* you."

He took off his hat. It had been a dam;
perspired rivers flowed
down his face when the dam was lifted.
He mopped his face with a handkerchief
embroidered with praying hands in the
corners that Mamalee could see.

"Ever hear of fire, Miz Jenkins? Ever hear of
something being in the bottle of medicine other
than what the doctor says is there? Ever hear of that?
How about you, Gal; what have you heard of?
F-i-r-e—you know what that spells, Gal?
Your death. Any word you spell out spells out
your death. Good Day, Miz Jenkins."

He waved his hat at Esmenda Dube who caught the door
so he didn't get the final sound
that would have made for him a powerful exit.
What came instead was Mamalee's favorite part.
Esmenda didn't like being threatened. So as
Ralph Littleton left, Esmenda called out after him
although she addressed Mamalee.

"Leticia Lee, since you've been accused, you might as well
learn something now. Every word does not spell 'death';
for instance, there's j-u-s-t-i-c-e which spells everything else."

After that, the widow kept getting
those headaches she hated, and they made her angry
instead of killing her so she got rid of her slaves.
She said she was sorry but she couldn't stand it.

Couldn't do it anymore. Ralph Littleton
was pressuring her in many ways,
trouble at the bank,
trouble at the store,
theft of her machinery,
barn fire,
daily disappearance of a chicken,
kerosene baths for her corn and
kerosene in her well. Little calling cards.

Esmenda decided slavery was giving her those headaches,
so she ran away. She had her husband's guns
and knew how to use them, used them better
than her husband who spotted game for her
to shoot at for big holiday suppers.

Should have used them on Ralph Littleton.
Should have given every student a gun and a book.

Mamalee said Esmenda first thought of using that gun
to defend what she was doing, but the little calling cards
became unbearable. She got rid of her slaves by leaving
them there, and leaving them an apology and a will.

Nobody in the county ever heard from Esmenda again.
Mamalee didn't say what happened to Esmenda's guns.

She also said that Esmenda Jenkins Dube
would have wanted a northern life,
as far north as north can be, limits of north
where it was so cold nothing there understood hellfire,
and the mountains were white, like full-hipped women
sleeping undisturbed, women of the cold clouds
breathing out more cold clouds that departed their mouths
when they whispered *heaven* in their northern dreams.

The Dube slaves weren't left alone.
Mr. Littleton returned and took away every book
he could find save the ones Mamalee hid well or could tuck
about herself. She wouldn't submit to a search
of her body, claiming she was a fool slave, fool enough
to kill herself a white man and call it a white elephant
she had bagged. "I don't know better than to do that,"
she said, "because I don't know nothing."
They didn't touch her.
Maybe she had a gun.

The county judge didn't care about the widow's will.
Said Mamalee wrote it.
Said Mamalee was a slippery one.
Instead of reporting right away
about the widow's desertion—or was it murder?

Judge Eaton kept needling her about
what she had done with the widow's pretty pink-faced
property—Mamalee, he said, was practicing

to make her writing look just like the widow's.
Called her a snake of a Negress forger.
Said it was best to get her out of
the great state of Tennessee as fast as possible.
Get her over to Louisiana down where the south
runs out of south. Deep, deep Alabama.
Best place for her; she was trouble's mother and
trouble's daughter. Said she'd be trouble's godchild, too,
if trouble had any undertaking with any kind of a god.

"There warn't no will," Judge Eaton concluded;
"nobody's emancipated," he added

and sat back for a week in the chair
(that Mamalee always sat in)
looking for something white
that was related to the widow

till he found a cousin so distant,
by way of Adam and Eve, he said, only the white
and a favor coming due

was related to the fraud
when he shook Peter Thomas Perry's
young inheriting hand

and Peter Thomas Perry sold
Leticia Lee's house and land
and added on
three more slaves
to his more arable Perrysburg
where Captain was called *Odysseus*
whom Mamalee already knew
from his many visits to her school
and to her to give her twin sons
—the only way he could pay for his education—
with his coppery Odysseus hair.
Master Peter liked that hair.

I was born within a year.

By being who she was
and not scared to be her
in front of the master
it was as if she said to him
she's staying just
because she wants to

as if she's thinking of herself as a guest

in what will be Leticia Lee's
magnificent boardinghouse
and companion enormous,
great odd bank account.

VISITING JESSPER AT STALEY FARM,
IN THE MIDDLE OF A BAD DREAM

Jessper, I just dreamed I was a luna moth emerging,
wings drying under the most potent moonlight
there ever was, ready to fly for the rest of my life
when the tail of my left hind wing tangled
in the silk I was leaving behind,

and though I was flying,
my green wings velvety yet shimmering
in that potency as if made of the sheerest silk
whose legend disappears on your fingers
just as the meanings of words vanish
under Ralls Janet's fingers;

though I was flying
as I always knew I would
because I just wouldn't not fly
despite my circumstance, after all,
the vocabulary of flight is mine,
and I know the meaning, my natural language,

but though I felt the air all around me
I was tethered; a luna moth kite
navigated by Peter Perry's hands winding the silk
tether of my split cocoon around his wrists
like a set of expensive cuffs.
One of a kind.

He walked me in that potent moonlight.
Walked me in a circle, walked me in a dance
he led.

———

Jessper held her arm out over the burning woodpile.

some flame tips were like moths themselves.
Some moths brown as her arm landed
near her wrist, males called females called males there.

She cupped her free hand over a moth
and through gaps between fingers
saw how active the wings were
beating against her palm,
the distress causing her no pain.
She shook the others free

and they rose to be the apex of the fire.

We like to see things rising. spent hours
watching smoke rise into vanishing. It looked
so easy. Ralls Janet had almost pulled it off;
almost vanished; she was already inconsequential,
sometimes you couldn't see her, could walk
right through her; all that was left for her to do
was finish fading.

Jessper held the moth up by its wings
as she might hold an open hymnal
if she ever were to hold one.

"What kind of moth is this, Varl?"

I studied it with my eyes. small thing.
Did it think itself fragile? Would it need to?

The moving fire moved shadows across the moth
like small clouds gathering, funneling into the wings.

I'd have to look in Master Perry's *Great Book
of Insectean Marvels* to get the name that
had been given to it

so I just told Jessper what I knew to be true
without research, "the kind that wants to be free."

Similar shadows funneled into Jessper's face.

"Is your Dob going to turn into a moth, too?"

I didn't answer her. Didn't want to put words to
what it would mean if he didn't, if he did.

Theodore Staley, Jessper's artisan of a master,
preferred physical amusement, didn't mind secret designs
and messages in private languages written on a slave's skin
(in locations usually covered)
with a lash; so practiced, he could cross the "T"
in anger's translation of Staley on Jessper's thigh
without looking
though she told me he looked.

Name raised in a larva of a welt.
My hand on it when I spoke.
"Let me teach you to read, Jessper."

She let the moth go. With wing damage,
the best it could manage was a gentler landing
than had it had no wings at all. Wings do turn ragged
in the old age of a few days. Some of the end
flying is at the former low altitude glide of shadows.

"I can't let you do that, Varl."

She started kicking dirt on the fire.

"Theodore Staley wouldn't have to know.
Keep it secret. Enjoy some secret power over him.
That's what it takes. He's turning you
into a mess of his secrets.
We'll just read to each other in the dark Sundays.
Your only book doesn't have to be scars
he gave you. You can get lost in his pages.
Write yourself a map out of them.
Once he's written on all of you, there won't be
any Jessper left."

"He would find it and read it.
He would turn my treasure into his own
and hurt me with it, burning me
with the fiery words of what I risked."

She pointed at the stars.
"What can you do about all his extra eyes?"

———

Moths blossom from the cocoon just to die
like any flowers picked
like any beauty too perfect to keep.
And that's the problem. To last would be
a defect of living. Maybe that's what
Peter Perry is searching for, a forever defect
because he needs that long to try to come to terms
with his sins. I amuse him and vex him
just as much. Life is too perfect to keep.
The whole system of slavery is too perfect
for the masters to keep. It is ideal

34

for them. Like those few precious luna days.
I want to blossom anyway, to prove
the wide world held inside.
I'm afraid, too; I would blossom out of fear.
I'd fly because my wings tremble intensely.
Jessper would wither on the vine,
let a stem swallow the flower,
let a neck swallow the head's whole
garden of thought.
We die so differently, me above the ground.

Luna moths like pale green clouds,
rain of precious pale green leaves
to bookmark Jessper's grave

that I dreamed of.

DOB

Dob's got a long bag strapped around the neck,
and he's bent down to count
the soft white money he's packing in it swiftly
as a thief, hunched down because he
doesn't like to brag his wealth.

Dob's so strong, he seems the king of strength
out there. The mile of sack follows him,
Dob's the leader,
like a hundred midget servants bleached and packed
so close together they seem to be all one weaving,
all one honoring of the king.

King of Unison, the country
where Dob will take a wife and live
the rest of his days

having to do nothing
because unison's doing it all.

I like the cotton
when Dob is the king
when Dob takes on ruling
over something

and does so much good for himself
and for the something. I like

how they both like to gleam,
Dob brighter.

It's as if he's not alive
unless he's ruling. Unless
his life is his kingdom
and he has stretched it to the clouds
he's scooping up.

I like
how Dob moves.

He's got muscles that seem to be
what wants to burst out the cotton pod
when it pops.

Look at the fire all around him
that every move he makes ignites.
A hat full of hot weather,
a storm of milk of every wiry dripping strand
of his hair.

Dob.

He keeps his path kingly
even though stepping on hulls, rocks, broken branches
doesn't feel that good, there is some pain, cuts, but
as it is kingly pain, he steps on, doesn't stop

as if he's putting on a show for everybody
who would like to see a king working with them.
But he's really showing himself something, thinking
about the throne in his head,
the throne the row he's picking leads to.
His fingers open up also
like the cotton.

I stop washing Ralls Janet's window
and practice for a minute how to best
fold my arms to be a throne.

I wash the window
about fifteen times to watch him,
and then I'm wanting a window like that myself
in the cabin
if that window
would always show me this picture.

I've been looking at him a lot and already
calling him *mine*, though if he was asked,
he likely would thank you kindly
then say how he'd prefer to be his own.

King.

I see the rolled backs of the pickers.
Some hired from Staley and Cheston farms;
not enough Perry labor to do it all.
(Some Staley payment in form of feeding and housing
Staley slaves overnight. Staley saves a lot
with this every night overnight practice.)
I see the roll. The curve I would want
for a roof. The curve like the top of an aster,
formed by arms, weary branches.

I see what looks like a sea of pregnant bellies
but they're rumps up as proud as flags.

Most times,
I'm out there flagging, too.

Will be
in just a minute

when I can give up
this picture.

Some minutes are longer than others,
Dob minutes; he's the king
of them, too. I fill some of my days
with them, my fullest days.

King of days.

SWEET ENOUGH OCEAN, COTTON

I haven't seen the sea before
but it must be easy to love

because even without ever seeing it before
I call the blown-open cotton a sea,
I call moving through the rows
my attempt to walk on rough water.

It's not that the cotton seems watery
or that each cotton seed hair is like
a separate one of the sparkles the sun makes
when its light bounces in moving water,

—though it is like that
now that I think about it.

It's just how big
the cotton is. This small field

seems bigger than the sky,
and is the sky for ants. It's just

how the cotton carries you,
delivers you on a rocky shore,
shipwrecks you,

strands you

even though you can't argue
against what good it does

because you have been taken up in
the persuasion of a garment, of a cocoon.

I've been thinking about this.
While I'm working, I think
about this. My mind is the part of me
that gets the least rest.

It's never quiet;
there's always the hum
inside me, the hive free inside me
making me think about honey, dipping
all my thoughts into honey

and even the thoughts honey won't
stick to have been in the honey,
have been next to honey so the knowledge
of honey is on them and the knowledge
all by itself can be sweet enough.

I think about that, think how thinking
can be sweet enough

for now. Thinking about, thinking about
so much that is buried in the cotton.

Few months after we planted it,
I called the pink blooms of cotton before it ripened
an assault of endless sunset on the ocean.

LUSA AND THE MUD MAN

Lusa Ralls Perry wanted to get dirty today
("This being *dirt day*, what slaves call *Thursday*
and why it's their favorite day," she said)
but discovered she couldn't get dirty
because dirt wouldn't stick
to her nearly nine years of pretty

and dirt so wanted, she boasted,
to stick to it. It was certainly reasonable
to me that Lusa would be privileged
that way, taken into dirt's confidence.
"Everything wants to be all stuck up on my pretty,"
she told me, having me walk around the yard,
doing her sunning for her. She would burn.
I belong to the child who belongs to the mother
who belongs to her husband
just as I do.
"Dirt was leaping and trying powerfully hard
to stick to me, but it couldn't do anything but fall
at my feet and get walked on while I was *at school.*"
Dwarf Sully drives her.

She's just a child I reminded myself,
precious-luna-moth of a child. Ralls Janet
would love Lusa better if Lusa were hers only.

Just me and her. Most everybody else off picking
apples (including some Ralls Janets), peanuts, pears.
Me and her. A child of Peter.
Peter in Kentucky; horses, seeing his corn
turned to whiskey.

"Show me how to make Nigra toast," Lusa said.
"I can't make it by myself; might burn myself.
And I'm much too rich to have to, even
if I didn't burn."

"Yeah, you are too rich, Lusa.".

"You better call me *Miss* Lusa."

"It would be better if you were gone
so that I could *miss* Lusa. You're always
around; I don't get a chance to miss Lusa."

"I like how you talk, Varl.
Why aren't you scared? You should be scared."

"Scared of words? I don't see why
anybody ought to fear words. Words are tools;
you have to know how to use them to get done
the job you want to get done. Can't do the work
if you're scared of the work.

If I were scared, I couldn't get you a cup of creek
water when you want one. Snakes pee in that creek
just as I told you, but I always suck that snake pee out
of the creek and spit it in the weeds before I dip
your cup in it. Couldn't do that if I were scared."

"You're not a real teacher, Varl.
You can't ever be a real teacher
so I don't want you to make so much sense
when you're talking to me. I order you
not to make sense."

"Can I make anything else?"

"Just so long as it's not sense, go on
and make it. Like that toast I asked for.
You toast yet, Varl? Have you made my toast yet?"

"It's just about burnt, the way you like it."

"How do you know what I like?
You can't get inside a white girl's mind.
But I suspect you want to. I suspect you'd rather
have a white mind and a white body to put it in. "

"No, I suspect I can't get in your mind.
You're right, Lusa. No way I can fit all of myself
into a white little girl mind."

"You trying to insult me?
You always try to insult me when you make sense.
I told you I don't like it."

"Not at all. I'm just trying not to make sense."

"Well, try some more harder, Varl. You're still
too close to sense. Mama says you can't ever be
as smart as I am even if I don't ever go to school
again."

"Your mama said no such thing. You probably had a dream."

"You inside Mama's mind, too? She wouldn't let you
in there. And I wouldn't waste a dream on you."

"You, *Miss* Lusa, brought up the subject of the mind."

"I don't like how you're saying that.
If you're laughing inside, I'll take care of you.
I know how to hurt you, if you make me hurt you.
You like Dob, don't you?"

"No; it wouldn't make any sense to like Dob;
Dob's not mine to like."

"If it doesn't make sense, then that's why you do it.
I gave you an order. And you like tricking people
that you're not making sense when you're making the most.
You like him. I know you like him. Everybody knows.
He knows it, too. But he doesn't like Nigra toast;
he always gets that to eat. He wants something special
like me. You laugh at me, I'll tell my papa
that Dob got me picked out to be his sugar toast
and then there won't be a Dob for you to like."

"You're too young to know about
that kind of scheming."

"I must not be, because I know it.
If it wasn't for me to know, then I wouldn't.
—Oh, I'm just fooling, Varl. I have fun with you.
I wouldn't do that; I just want you to remember
that I could do it anytime I want to,
but without Dob, you wouldn't be much fun.
And you would retallgate."

"You mean *retaliate*, don't you?"

"No. I mean whatever I said."

"I'm supposed to help you."

"Not with talking. Not with words
you're not supposed to know.
You're supposed to do for me what
I don't want to do."

"I know. But I thought you didn't want
to speak properly, so I did."

"That doesn't make sense. Sure I want to
speak properly so folks can understand
what I'm saying. You understood me."

"It's hard not to."

Lusa laughed her nearly-nine-year-old laugh.

"It's going to be my birthday soon.
There's something I always wanted to do, and now
I'm about too old for it. You help me do it,
Varl. Cover me up with mud.
I want to see if you can really breathe when
all that dark is crowding your skin. You must
be on the verge of collapsing any minute."

"That's from working too long in the heat,
not from having black skin."

"Cover me with mud, Varl."

"Wait till it rains. Then you can just bellyflop
around the yard. You'll be the opposite from
a snake; it slides skin off, you'll slide skin on."

"Cover me, Varl. If you put the mud on me,
I can stay out in the sun without a hat.
I won't burn with a mud coat on. Protect me

with the mud, Varl. You have to do it.
I'm ordering you."

"Wait till later; mud will be muddier later."

"*Now*, Varl."

"Very well. But I've got to get
these velvet butter beans picked. These tomatoes
and squash. Got to get some eggs and butter
out the springhouse. There's not time
for your mud, but very well. Eat mud cakes
tonight."

I walked off from her not finding a taste
for any more oddity. Not finding in myself
her father's complicated incurable indulgence.
There's probably mud science. There are probably
scientists who devote all their time to studying mud
and finding muddy medicine. It might be good
for Lusa to wear a mud skin. She's not seeking
that good, but it might be good anyway. What do I
know about how peculiar goodness can be
seeing as how slavery is taken for good by so many?

The bullfrogs by the creek have, on both sides
of their throats, thin skins that inflate like sails
that are wind gorged.
A bullfrog's throat sails don't inflate every time
the frog breathes, just when it sings
from what I've noticed, but I'm not sure why, maybe
the female frogs like the oddity of it, and look
at it the way I look at Dob, and the better

the bullfrog inflates his throat bubbles,
the more likely that she will be his love,
there's competition, but I'll have to observe this more,
really study
after it more before I can say surely. I am now sure,
for instance, through daily study I have determined
that Peter Perry is starting to love me with intent
to romance only what is deviant about me. I'll keep on
watching him.

So Lusa wants dark skin. That's all right. I'm glad
it can be chosen by someone who doesn't
have to choose it. I like to think that I would choose
my teabark if I had to choose a color. I like to think

I would choose it not because I know I don't really
have a choice, and I'm just trying to make the best
of what I'm stuck with, but because of how it appeals
to my eye and how warm a color it is, how full
it seems to be of honey that makes it easier to eat

lots of things that would be otherwise without
easy flavor. The perfect palatability of sweet
on top of vicious choices. That's what the honey
of my teabark does for Peter Perry, too, gives him
the delicacy of slavery.

The approaching sunset
was not honey color, but it put everything
in honey light. Everything glowed
in the final honey-illuminated hours.

Lusa had taken off her clothes while I pumped
water and filled the washtub, dug up and added dirt.
She didn't realize what that looked like, little
naked white girl standing there

in a thoroughly diminished nakedness.
There it was, the reason for scourge
thoroughly unable to impress me
with its exposure. Like something
out of the womb too soon.
Something incomplete.

Her skin looked to be too smooth
for something to grab hold of her.
Your hands would slide right off
unless you grabbed her by the hair. By the
broom-wheat hair. Albino Pearl's hair was like that, too,
it belonged to her and she to Master Perry
who hoped she'd have an albino baby
for his collection.
Pearl gets hired out to a Chickasaw.
My father is hired out to Rouper-Adler Shipyards.

I stirred up some mud, big pot of mud much like
a batch of too-thin molasses. Liquid Lusa picture
of me, a Varl giving in to trepidation.
Except the batch empty of that smell that
has nothing sweet about it when its old.
Smells a bit of root, rot, slop, a bit of licorice
growing not far from where the stream separates
into three long, thin, drying up fingers
and disappears till it rains.
These are sorghum days. The time of needing
to make everything taste better by covering it up.

I started to smear mud all over Lusa, using sticks
and leaves to spread it, but the leaves tore up
in my hands and pieces of green stayed to the top
of the mud here and there on Lusa. As if maybe
frogs didn't have ears because here they were

anchored in Lusa's mud skin. Finally,
I just put the mud on her with my hands.
It didn't look much like skin.
She wasn't going to learn much about being black
from this mud, just about being muddy, but I
didn't say so. I saved her feet, ankles, four inches
of leg and a circle of stomach with her navel in the center
like the dark circle in the center of an eye,
for last. She seemed to be wearing white stockings.
I could've left her white-gloved
like her mama usually was but didn't think to.
This was good enough. Plenty good enough.

I was liking much how it progressed. My sculpture
was alive, one of a kind; maybe I could get a deal
going with Master Peter and earn some money (a business
arrangement different from the one we already had,
one with a contract, consent, mutual agreement).
I decided to talk to my artwork just like,
I realized, how some artists might think
something similar to what I was thinking
when they made a black bird
out of tar, feathers, and a man.

"You ever hear about those muddy slave graves
over in Landry, Miss Lusa? Don't speak
unless you want a muddy tongue and muddy teeth, too.
I'm willing if that's what you want, but keep the lips
tight sealed if you don't. Just shake your head.
Anyway, over in Landry, the slave bodies weren't buried
deep enough

or something.—I see you're shaking your head.
You think they *were* buried deep enough?
You're disputing the facts?
Oh, you're shaking it more wildly—the black

must be taking effect quickly. No? Oh, *Landry*;
you never heard of *Landry*? Well, of course not;
Landry's gone now, on account of what happened
when the slave bodies weren't buried deep enough.
Science could verify this, but even science
keeps away from Landry.

The river flooded and the bodies started rising.
It looked like the love of revenge, the start
of deviant or righteous justice, depending on
who you talked to,
and the master that buried his slaves there
would have turned white from the shock if
he could have turned any whiter.
His heart stopped and stayed stopped

just long enough for his wife to believe
he was dead, and even though he came back,
she thought it was a dead man coming back to her.
She treated him just as if he was dead.
Everybody over in Landry treated him
as if he was dead. As if evil presided
over Landry. He is dead now though.
All of Landry's dead."

"Why you telling me that? Doesn't have a thing
to do with giving me a dark day." She tried to spit out
all the mud.

"Well, if you say it doesn't, then I guess it doesn't.
But it is interesting about that mud
and those dead slaves.
It was definitely the darkest day in Landry.
It was as if the dead bodies had turned to mud
trying to get back to meaningful flesh.
I don't know but that when the mud hardens on you,

you'll find yourself inside somebody.
It'll be just as if you were eaten. The mud man
will use your body to be his new body for his
life's second chance. I don't know but that
that's what it'll be like. You'll be his white mind
inside him."

"That makes no sense at all."

"The mud man's counting on that attitude.
That attitude helps him control that white mind
inside him, and then it's his."

Lusa stretched out her arms and examined them.
Licked her little mud lips.

"I like it. It's better than I thought it would be,
seeing how it's black skin I'm trying on.
Slaves don't really need to wear clothes
because you always wear your color;
to be naked you'd have to take your black off.

Look at us, Varl; we're twins!

It's much easier to make me black than to make
you white. I'm you now, Varl. And I'm
going to be you when you tell Dob that you
can't stand him."

It was a good time to stuff her throat with mud,
or wish the mud into tar, but for what?
She doesn't think much of people if she can so easily
stop being herself to become somebody else.
I can't even switch my name
easily, even though I know the name I use isn't
my name. Mamalee wasn't planning on naming me

after her master's horse.
She was going to call me *Free*. Not that I wouldn't
get around to calling myself that even if no one else
did. That's what I have become under Luna cocoon-cover.

Lusa was admitting to me
that she wasn't much at all, nothing
of consequence, nothing to take seriously
or to take any way at all.
Besides, if she really was me
she would not have said that.

She also said you don't find much in nature
that can make you white. That's why it's so special
to be white. That's why.

That's why, too,
I don't like her

unless she's in a mud coffin
like the one she told me
to put her in.

But she's just a child.
Remember that, Varl. What's Free
in the cocoon might not want to,
might not have to.

The Lord loves
an innocent child.

What about the ones who aren't innocent?

The right amount of water
thickens dirt to get-by soup.

Too much water
washes dirt down to
brown blood flowing;
a dirty river
bleeding to death.
Lusa said it's hard

not to find dirt
if you're looking where dirt is.

She was right about that. Me and Mamalee
always have to clean the Perry house.
Every few days I wash Lusa, too.

My thinking made me miss some of what Lusa
had been saying, but my attention returned to her
in time to hear her tell me that I didn't have to wash
as much because it took longer for dirt to cake up on me
and make it look as if there was something on me
that could be scraped off, that could come off.
Dirt blends in, feels at home, but not everybody
can make something feel welcome.
Ralls Janet can't get used to her own house
though everybody opens the doors for her.

Suddenly, the mud screamed
as it left my hand for Lusa's face.

"You slapped me," she accused
just as she was welcome to do

because I knew I didn't do it.

"The mud man slapped you, Lusa.
I tried to stop him
but he had a reputation to protect,
and he was protecting it from you."

54

I had to wash the mud off her, but not till after
Ralls Janet saw her muddied daughter and thought
I'd taken the authority of my writing
with her husband's ink and switched it
to writing with tar.
"What have you done, Varl?"

"Can't you tell, Ralls Janet? You don't have
to read words to figure this out; it's nothing
but a picture of your daughter as she might look
if I was her mother and your husband was her father,"

was what I felt like saying, so I'm stitching it in
to be like it was actually stated.

"Following Lusa's orders," I said without looking up;
Ralls Janet could have been just a breeze, her question
just the breeze sounds moving without purpose through
the leaves.

I had hoped to be through with the mud
before they got back
from the small stand of fruit trees, Ralls Janet
liking the Ralls Janet apples,
but my hope wasn't sincere or I would've hurried.

"Anything else? You seem to want to say more."

"I thought you had laid tar on her."

"I wouldn't do that. If you told me to,
I wouldn't do that."

Like any good teacher, I wanted Ralls Janet
to see the importance of limits.

She wanted me beaten. Since no one moved,
she had to wait for her husband's order.
He didn't give it, preferring a higher oddity,
Her face red as a Ralls Janet apple.

Maybe later I'll tell her I was practicing
how to make that Master Book I might be writing
when I'm Free, a book the master would like
if he could be alive to see it,
his skin cut up and turned into the pages.
My experiment.

He'd really appreciate
something like that.

The corrupt intimacy.

Maybe she would, too,
as long as it was limited
to him. But it wouldn't be for her.

THE P OF WATER

The sun rose right above Peter Perry's house looking
from the slave cabin Ralls Janet ordered, roof splitting
the early light
to fall all around the house like vines.
As day got going, while I was sewing
for Ralls Janet and her daughter Lusa Ralls;
the shadow of the house grew
and like a whale swallowed the cabin.

A sign as sure as any that I shouldn't be here.

Middle of the day, Dob and Dwarf Sully finished diverting
the creek so that through Perry fields, the water
would flow in a P.

Twisted water
suits him.

Ralls Janet sulked in the window
her hair loose and around her like preparation for mourning.
Like the cascade of light around the house.
Mamalee had been diverting, too, and gathering honey,
scraping it off the comb into a bucket, Peter Perry standing
right behind her like a bear.
She walked out the woods some evenings

a few minutes after him. Her voice deeper, raspy,
since she was kicked in the throat some years ago
by a horse.
She read to him in soothing small thunder.
Romance was all language, Ralls Janet thought, the secrets
in books. She would prefer if there were touching
between them, if he were taking advantage

of Mamalee as was his privilege,
but in this they were both violating her.

Deforming Ralls Janet's existence.

I would not be willing to trade places with Ralls Janet.

She was so pale she could have been moonlight.
So unable to grasp anything. Just able to shed
some of her light on other things, giving others
something to read better by. Just able to shed,
diminish during a month.

I can bear being a slave better than I can bear
the nasty details of her life. What did she think about
in her miserable hours? How often did she accuse herself
of being what little she was? Would she know
how to choose something besides which piece of chicken
to fork off the platter?

Ralls Janet was not my responsibility.

I've thought more and more about leaving
and I hadn't told anybody, because the more who knew
of my plan the more dangerous it would be. There was only three
who needed to know anyway. Jessper who would never run
from the Staleys whose farm was the closest to the Perrys
and just a little further north, in the right direction.
I talked the most to her (and Dob) , but she was easily
frightened and I couldn't trust her fear. Trouble knew her
about as well as I knew her. Maybe better.

Mamalee of course, and it would be the hardest to leave her.
Dob because I love him, but maybe he'll run, too.
He thinks about it. I see it in his eyes, and in the hard way
he hits the earth as if to kill it with a hoe.

Running away would be another way of saying
what the cloth pages of my cocoon are saying, and what
I'll have to do when I break out of the cocoon that is
thickening nicely
in strategic places under my dress.
I realize that since it is a cocoon, I'll have to break out
one day. It is an expectation of a cocoon.

I feel so bold wearing my thickening writing. I keep hoping
for frisky breezes to open and lift the outer loose dress
so that Ralls Janet can see what's taking shape under it,
words all over me, strength and braces. One day when
we're hanging wash to dry, breeze could come
like an invisible chariot. She joins in with the laundry,
and we're each other's silent company. She wants to talk,
really needs to talk.
She was only eight years older than me.
In sunlight, I looked more radiant, yellow creeping
into my brown, turning me
into color of a perfect dome of new bread
(she'd love to take a knife to
and would be able to only if I were bread).

She was often beside me, drawn to me, loathing me,
envying me, wanting, always wanting
to talk to me. Trust me. I don't know what a life
without trusting something would be like. If nothing else
I trust my assessment, my judgement of things.
Who did she have?
Peter Perry? Mamalee? Eveline Staley, an invalid
that Jessper tended?
She was far from her Virginia relatives.
Far from her Maryland cousins. I was surrounded
by everyone who loved me
(except my father).

More and more now, I am afraid
of how Peter Perry might find what's underneath
and remove me from the cocoon himself, delighted
with the rich enormity of my defect. Would he fold
my luna wings? The rarity of their being the size they are
to get me off the ground? Would he snatch them off my body?
Reshape them to carry his profile in the air? Or would he risk
damaging his prize specimen? Would he just lock me in a glass case
and stare until he believed in the miracle of his experiment?

I can't be like Jessper who seemed like such a good slave;
I don't care if I seem good or not. That kind of good
is not in me. Not since I've been in my cocoon.

And I can't be like Mamalee
who runs a secret school for slaves and provides a place
for traveling men to rest and eat between gathering news
and guiding runaways to safe places. Caves among
the hills and mountains. Much wild fruit. Warm stuff
from her hearth if they need it. Most do.
Peter Perry's non-interference if in fact he knew.
Ralls Janet would sell her soul for this information
then she'd sell that to get her soul back. Ralls Janet
is the danger.
Mamalee couldn't do this if she wasn't in slavery.
The whole thing she lives for would be ruined
if she wasn't in slavery.

That's something I just don't want to believe.
How deformed the sense of that is.

I can't be satisfied with the education
of slaves, with revenge of the mind
like Mamalee.

And there was the matter of Peter Perry himself,
the secret something between him and Mamalee
that I didn't really want to understand. To carry on
that way
with an enemy, to give the dark honey of your voice
to the one who sent away your husband, who was involved
in the disappearance of your sons.
—I couldn't do all that she does with him.

I live for something else
pupating in my cocoon.

It's almost like I'm the master.
And then I'd belong to him more than ever.
Two of a kind.

There's no better life possible in being owned
until the only thing that owns you is life itself
That's why Peter Perry can't be good to me
as long as he can call himself my master
and make me call him that
and calls me anything he wants to but *Free*
the name Mamalee wanted to give me
but he put *Varl* in the ledger instead, same number of letters
but a world of difference in meaning, *Varl* being as far
from *Free* as he had the power to put me,
hurting me worse than if he would hit me.
I just can't stop thinking about that deforming of power.
The only grace there is, is in the beauty of these
intricate stitches.

What would I be thinking about
if I didn't have to belong to slavery?
I have to give up all the possibilities of life
for having to focus
on being a slave and on becoming free.
Staying free.

It's similar for the masters who have to focus
on keeping slaves enslaved so that they have something
to be the master of; there's really not much point
in claiming to be the master over cotton or hogs.
That's why Ralls Janet has such a hard time mistressing;
she's not even the mistress over words, can't read or
write or impress her husband who is also her master
with her thinking. Won't let her learn. She was placed
above learning. As long as she could recognize
the name *Perry*.
She was so lonely. So unrecognized.
But not my responsibility.

What great things are not happening
because of all this misplaced concentration?

Maybe I'll go pee in the P of water.

THE COMFORT WHALE

Any way that you were connected to a master
was a sad way. Ralls Janet married one.

What were slaves supposed to do about it?
What were slaves supposed to care about it?
We belonged to them; they didn't belong to us.
My master wasn't really   mine.

Ralls Janet had white gloves for wearing to church
and town, to up the esteem for her husband
when she traveled with him, rarely, to Nashville
or Kentucky for new exploits and business opportunities,
like the special soap he had us make from the fat
of deformed animals. There was a kick to the clean
from that. He liked to take Pearl, his albino,
and Sully, his dwarf, and get money off
of letting people look at them, touch them. Covered up
in the wagon till he was paid.

Instead, Ralls Janet wore her gloves almost all the time.
Yet they didn't seem to get dirty, as if the work she did
had no effect on things
(they weren't rich enough yet—but climbing—without
a much anticipated shipping inheritance—despite
the stipend from Aunt Baly-Belinda,
for Ralls Janet not to work, too—some—didn't have
enough slaves, couldn't at that time afford more
without depleting his profits was what he told her
when she complained about not living as she should.
I think she just meant the reversal of elevation, me above her.
In truth, Peter Perry just couldn't find enough strange ones.
He managed to afford everything else he wanted.).

It was as if Ralls Janet couldn't exert meaning
from any of her actions. When she pulled the gloves off,
you expected her to pull off her hands, too.
As if nothing was connected to her wrists but gloves.

As if the gloves were her external floppy bones protecting
some even weaker white flesh that was entirely vulnerable
to every assault; rain just being playful, meaning no harm,
unless refreshing was harmful, ended up slicing into flesh
and washing away the blood at the same time. She had

fingers that knew nothing about defense, not even
about scratching, digging into, and grabbing hold
of something. Though she worked.
She didn't keep anything sacred,
and I had to. Fingers like wet paper.
Her fingernails were like ice candy,
always about to melt, so she didn't let them warm up
to anything, and she stayed as cold as she could.
Took baths, too

in the gloves, in fact, was getting ready to take one
in this water I had just pumped, and then the gloves stuck
to her skin just like that skin wrapped around
a cooked egg, that skin between
the shell and the egg that was cooked so smooth
you wouldn't mind a face like that.

Only luna moth wings could be paler than her face.

With the gloves off, it was her hands that seemed flat
and empty, not the gloves that had captured the substance
of her sad business. I was watching

sadness seep through the gloves,
sadness soak the gloves.

She could wring so much sadness out of them
it would be as if she was milking, just as if
she was milking. But there's better milk than sadness.
You never had to turn to sadness
when you needed milk. Sadness

leaked out the gloves as if she'd got
her hands all stuck up in rain clouds.

Such a

sad woman.
Sad house.

Her bath water
was milky from her sadness when
she got out of it.

I noticed how paint curled to fall off
the sad white house
looked like the mistress' white fingers
falling off. That's how
a sad house cries,

how sadness replaced everything the house
was made of, sad wood, joints, sad shingles.
Sad bed Captain made.
She was standing there, a sad woman there
by the butterfly weed and rags, now, of pasqueflowers
and cried with the house that was just as sad.

Cried her fingers off. Stood
thumb-deep in tears. In flowers off their stems.
I worked around her. Like a bee. Like a big part
of what stung her.

Dwarf Sully was smiling, wiping his hands on his shirt,
he and Pearl out plowing out weeds since before sun.
She didn't take on color after hours in the sun.
Took on blisters. Peter Perry was fascinated.

Sully's squinting eyes seemed
like a smile above the other one
as if the sadness happening to Ralls Janet was his candy,
as if being a slave had killed his sympathy, and that
was dangerously deformed, too, to lose the ability for sympathy, to
get pleasure
out of misfortune no matter whose it was,

just about as dangerous as Mamalee or me
prizing defiance in the open. One day

her defiance might not amuse Master Peter anymore
but will annoy the master (as it already does the mistress
who is of no consequence), and on that day, he
might finally take action against it. How long
can something last?

Dwarf Sully's smile was noiseless; he'd found peace in his
enjoyment, whether proper or improper enjoyment,
of her sadness. This peace he'd found relaxed
Dwarf Sully's watchfulness. His smile seemed to take him out

of the truth of his situation
and that was supposed to be impossible;
the truth is not supposed to free you from the truth,
just from everything else. But he was smiling himself
out of the truth of his situation, and by doing so

he was coming near to smiling himself into
a white liberty with Ralls Janet.
He'd better watch out!

He'd better beware of how close he was coming
to a white liberty black men couldn't take
and live to say they took it
or live to even deny they took it
if they were caught
if they were accused of taking
what they didn't take.

Ralls Janet was just standing there, unmindful of Sully,
a man too little to matter, a life so inconsequential,
unmindful of the water I sloshed more so she could hear it
and notice. Dwarf Sully's smile deepened,
and seemed to me to move him
closer to that white liberty

without his even becoming aware of how he was moving
closer to it. When he realized how close he was
getting to it, he'd be there, already inside the liberty,
like how you caught sickness just standing there
and not trying to catch it. When he knew how close
he was to it, he'd already be reaching for her hand,
maybe just to snatch off that glove and see if anything
was really under the linen, but the reaching
would look like something else, might
even feel like something else, to her, to him, to both
of them.
Maybe he'd catch himself and remember how he got his name
(for being black as dirt, for being blasphemy
against God as dwarfs just had to be,
his naming former owner said)
and would drop his hand back to the plow
instead of reaching further for Ralls Janet's hand

whether to love it
whether to harm it
whether to save it.

He was too close to taking a white liberty
he wasn't free to take. It was time for him
to back away, turn tail and run, hide
out in one of the caves in the mountains
with the Cherokees who wouldn't walk away west.
Refused removal.
Rock walls might block
the white liberty with the mistress.
The white liberty

that could start with removal of her title, calling her
Ralls Janet, as I do, instead of calling her *Mistress*.
Calling her an endearment. *Honey. Sunshine-Sugarcake.*
Title so like a bandage that when it was gone exposed
a way for contact to happen; in its place
what seemed like a sturdy bridge that wanted

his skin getting to hers

—and it was pretty, made
a marvelous design (fit for Master Peter's book)
when their fingers interlocked, Dwarf Sully's knuckles
like coal hills, his fingers like black logs
sliding down the iced ponds of her nails;

checkerboard, white and
black moves first

I wanted to see that, for real, pretty as it was
in my mind, and in my mind nothing like
a white liberty at all, but if it wasn't confined
all to my mind, and Sully took her hand, and if
she didn't welcome it
or if they were caught,

then I couldn't call it a lovely experiment
if he took her hand and undressed it, snatched
off the glove, and I didn't want to know what
the death of Dwarf Sully was. I hoped
Sully didn't want to know that yet either,
I hoped he didn't decide to die for this liberty
with a white woman
instead of for the liberty of being a man
as he was with Mamalee.

There was no liberty permitted a slave.
No kind of liberty that was sanctioned

even if the black tried to refuse
violation (it happened both ways)
and tried to retaliate, the traveling men said
when they were here last night.

Dob walked off
while the traveling men were talking, so I doubted
he heard the end of the story or figured it was too easy
to predict it. Story of a girl his age at the end
of it, my age at the beginning. Dob walked
toward the trees, and I watched
till his shadow was lost among them.

Last night two traveling men told about one
Clarie Lukton, a Missouri black girl who killed
the master Lukton for trying to force himself on her
once again, just as he had done from the day
he bought her, forty miles away, before he could even
get her all the way home where he was building her
a proper cabin. His wife had died

some years ago, and his two daughters ran the house, one
older than Clarie, one younger. The traveling men said
that according to the census there were many
white Missouri women of age and without men
whom Lukton could have outright married,
four of them closer than the forty miles
he had to travel to purchase Clarie,
and any of those aspiring wives would have been
at least a little more willing to be with him
than Clarie was

and maybe the white Missouri woman that would've
married him would've been upset enough, and resourceful
enough, unlike Lukton's daughters, to stop

a master's long night sessions
with his only slavegirl, and maybe with more and more
slavegirls as he continued to prosper.
All sober hours

given over to Clarie, too,
no strong drink to excuse
the inexcusable.

Just his, I figured I had to call it, preference
to explain his uninvited visiting of Clarie, though he
might have called it his right
to his property, to know everything about it.
And maybe out of respect
for an idea of white women he wanted to uphold,
he didn't want to ever approach them the way
that he approached Clarie

even though he called himself clean
when he came to her any time he wanted,

no matter what she was doing or whom she was trying
to be with, and to fall in love with. No wonder
Dob didn't want to hear it. No wonder it made
him so angry that Peter Perry started to look to him
like Lukton all dead and burned in Clarie's hearth.
Dead and burned in my hearth.

Dob was good with wood, carpenter coming on better
than the teacher who'd been Dwarf Sully
now that Captain, master carpenter, was gone
seeing other worlds. Why would he want to come back
to this deformity? Adler ships went everywhere,
to China, Italy.
Dob went out to the woods with his knife (can you believe
it? Peter Perry allows that against the rules,
Dob's own knife!, oddity of brute strength not being brutish
against the master. Ralls Janet incensed by this)
to work on carving Peter Perry's dark-deformed image.
Dob stayed the rest of night

carving in darkness "that even the blind can see"
he told me in the morning, his feelings still blazing,
he said, "like I had swallowed a thousand suns."
And what could that image of the master do in the face
of a thousand suns but what the thousand wanted?

I understand. Work for the master claims about all
the daylight, so if you have your own work, you have
to swear off sleeping.
I stitch through the night Dob carves.

I found myself wondering if their father's
interest in Clarie
made Lukton's daughters even more skeptical
about marriage? I wondered if their father's interest

made them unwilling to marry someone who kept female
slaves, especially young, pretty
(no use pretending they're not) ones? I wondered
if Clarie had started them thinking and scheming?
I wondered

if someone like Clarie explained why one of Lukton's
daughters was no longer married? If her husband
was dead, I wondered if maybe he had died from
either a wife's or a slavegirl's rage?

I wondered could Jessper kill her Master Staley
if she had to, if she valued herself enough?
I wondered if I could kill Peter Perry, really make
a master book?

I wondered about the possibility of experiments.

Clarie had more babies
than Lukton's married daughter had,
and Clarie's were Lukton's daughters' other
sisters and brothers.

I figured that his daughter must have struggled
with being married
just as her father had struggled with being married,
but father and daughter were each committed
to something else, she to decency

though that marriage was failing, too, as
maybe she began to feel
some satisfaction about her father's slavegirl
losing honor a slavegirl wasn't as slave
supposed to have.

Nothing decent should have been Clarie's, perhaps
the daughter reasoned, reluctant to blame her father
for a lack of control or respect for a womanhood
that came maybe before you were ready

to have something like that
so hard to defend, depending on who you were and
where you were and how willing you were not to act
like a lady.

My cocoon gives me added womanhood
because of where I add it under my dress.
Where I deliberately add it.
Is my thinking deformed?

Lukton's daughter might have learned to appreciate
Clarie's loss of honor
as a way to disguise her own helplessness
in influencing the head of the household's actions
and decisions; that could

have happened, judging by how Ralls Janet felt,
her resentment
over minutes between her husband and Mamalee
though all Mamalee and Master Peter did was read
and talk (far as I know), find words

he lost with Ralls Janet, and lost with her also
the impulse
or whatever it was that made a person speak
past the politeness that hadn't got enough meaning

to speak of.

Her greater resentment over me, that she can't contain
at all anymore, not even a self-dignifying half-hearted pretense,

her husband slipping, too,
as he lets his curiosity escalate
into caring for me as he should for her. How dangerous
my situation is becoming.

Clarie Lukton felt her womanhood was hers
and found lawyers who agreed
so took her defense of murder as prevention
of another assault
to county court and took her appeal
of her conviction and scheduled execution
to the Supreme Court

before accepting failure.

She did not die
Lukton's way, the body alive
but nothing else, the death of the rest of her
(death of pride, will, hope, love, joy, triumph)
probably celebrated by her master.

She did not die his way.

She had had enough. I don't know why
the day that seemed different to her seemed
different. I don't know what allowed Clarie
to reject aggression she had accepted
so many times before.
But something allowed for her to refuse.
And the something must be how she saw things.
The day must have given her new eyes to see the new sun
and to see what the new sun shined on, what the new sun
hadn't shined on before. Roof splitting the light
all around the walls. Ropes of light
to pull her out of there. Ropes of light

to weave into an impenetrable cloak.
Cocoon of light.
But if how she saw things, maybe just how
she saw herself, hadn't changed, what else could have?

As the traveling men told it, she just refused
to let him touch her so brutally ever again.
She found in herself emancipation
that let her act in a way that was
hard for her to choose or she might have killed him
sooner, a year or two sooner. Or a day.
But as soon as somehow
she saw a self in herself, she refused.

I would do that, too,
I hope,

lock up my house, offer
no master key

and I think about this, think
instead of sleep
about footsteps toward the cabin,
lamp flickering
through the trees

coming closer
—wildcat eyes!

never seemed to behold to praise.

I wonder if there was too much in the way
of master and slave, mistress and slave love,
for anything trying to be love   to be love?

I wonder if it always had to be something else
when you said *love* inside of slavery?
If instead of loving one you have to love two,
Jonah and the whale that swallowed him,
the one you loved
and the slave, the master, the mistress

that swallowed the one you loved.

My master loves me.

THE TENNESSEE BEEHIVE PROPHET PROJECT

Irene Perry, Peter Perry's grandmother, died yesterday,
sleeping on her grandson's porch, her mouth wide open
and so sweet of Tennessee whiskey
that it was full of bees when they found her.

Her tongue was so stung, so swollen
that Sully couldn't close her mouth. Bees
went in and out of her like crazy needles dancing
instead of stitching that mouth shut.
It was allowed for Sully to touch her dead, his
job, since he was a dwarf involved with all the dead,
mostly slave dead here and at the Staleys, the Cheston
and the Kelster farms, and animal dead not fit
for eating.

Doc Wallace Lonton said that
Irene must have been inviting the bees in for hours
because they had had time to set up a hive
in her throat
and turn some of her spit to honey
and tuck a queen in under Irene Perry's
thick quilt of a tongue.

She would have been left that way, the survivors
thinking on a miracle
except for the problem of a miracle
being served up by bees, and the problem of stingers
not being the acknowledged property of heaven
for being so much like the two points of the devil's
divided tongue,
but rot didn't stand for that anyway
and eventually got even more involved with the corpse
than the bees.

Rot didn't get there right away though;
Peter Perry's idea was faster. Beat grief, too.
He loved the hive Irene had become,
and the added spectacle
of a dwarf pursuing that mouth honey.
Albino Pearl filling the jugs.
Master Peter wrote up several signs
and invited people as far as Gallatin, Knoxville,
and Nashville, even got word to Roanoke,
to come see the miracle, come see the source
of his graces: a grandmother
who had become a fountain of honey.

The amazing, mystifying, miraculous honeyfying body
of Irene. The gold mine in every one of his pockets.

Too perfect to keep.

Come early
and see rivers of honey pour from her ears,

come fill
a jug with Perry Paradise Honey for a dollar.

He almost lost himself and nearly kissed me
he was so happy.

He forgot all about having to have a funeral.
Unless that's what all this spectacle was
(death of the last of the meaning of his marriage, too),
so many fine coins in Peter Perry's pockets.
Forgot to notify Aunt Baly-Belinda,
his grandmother's daughter-in-law.

Doc Wallace Lonton certified the death
and Rev. Lucious Adler (of the aristocratic Adlers
who made a fortune in whiskey, a family
into which Peter Perry's Aunt Baly-Belinda married,
wealth that therefore didn't touch Peter Perry directly
though he wanted it to, and tried to divert it
to himself just as he diverted that creek,
by being as sweet to Baly-Belinda as honey
and a son to her, called her *Aunt Mama* and everything);
Rev. Lucious Adler certified the miracle.

The certifier could tell that Irene's mouth
was open to praise and bless when the bees came in
like little angels in their best yellow-striped Sunday suits
and made the honey of heaven
that they were painting her soul with
and turning on the light of her soul with.
Rev. Adler called it the *Honeyfication of Irene*.

And that soon became the title of his most requested sermon.
(Peter Perry felt he was entitled to a percentage
of the collection on those Sundays, seeing as his own
Irene made possible Rev. Adler's fame.)

Some of the honey sticking to the little angel bee legs
rubbed off on Irene's tobacco-brown teeth
as the angel bees flew in and out
of Irene's transfiguring honeyfying body
and gave her teeth the appearance of each one of them
being a gold-rimmed, pearly, tobacco gate.

Angels touched you without being seen,
luna moths flew into the cabin, my dream of freedom
acting as a flame. I could feel the tails of luna hind wings
tickling my eyelids, but by the time I opened my eyes
they were gone.

They woke you up before the day got up
so you could splash cold spring water on your face
like you were being saved every morning
like you were waking up to a new world
and the only sound was a bird's sound,
only hammer was a woodpecker's
and that was all the time you got to be a person
because in a minute came the rest of it.

Varl, you heard *Varl*, and it was the magic word
that turned you back to slave.

Perry angels were bees. Varl angels
were luna moths. Desperation was both of ours.

Heaven in hives; heaven in cocoons.

More of it in the gold mines in his pockets.
Also his golden curiosity helping him see gold in me.

Peter Thomas Perry married Ralls Janet
when I was about five years old
(I don't remember much about the wedding
and now I'm about the age she was
when she married him) just for a dowry
which was mostly the prestige of marrying a Heffring
(she the prestige of getting closer to Adler money)
but since the wedding, the Heffrings have lost
almost everything but their color—and Ralls Janet lost
more of her flimsy hold on her husband—crop
and livestock sickness cleaned up their big farm pastures
and orchards to just sunlit, moonlit glow,
deformed all their plans; Ralls Janet
had once been a Heffring queen, had ruled; everything
gone except some faith, I suppose, which was mighty
difficult to put in a bank and was a paltry inheritance, too,

considering, for instance, that Jessper had more faith
(things would change, slavery might end in her lifetime)
than Peter Perry and Ralls Janet combined,
yet Jessper wouldn't ever take that enormous faith
and run with it to a place where faith and freedom
meant the same real thing
instead of dependency on miracles.

Rev. Adler was involved with whiskey, too,
but his involvement could be brought on entirely
by birthright and not sin
since he was born into the Adlers,
cousin to the founders of the Adler Distillery
and owners of the distillery's fortune that built
his magnificent church

where Dwarf Sully was two nights ago fixing the roof
that was damaged by gusts of wind that seemed
to take freedom more seriously than most of us.

Peter Perry's Aunt Baly-Belinda knew something
about freedom, too, about independence
and when she married into the Adlers, she set up
her nephew Peter as a supplier of some of
the distillery's grain, lifting Peter's spirit
(and his purse close to as much as he wanted
but he can't give up cotton, can't give up slaves, none
of his pleasure, can't give up a connection to Mamalee
as her master, only as her master, and through her,
reach me. He was a man of conviction but not of courage.
I saw him trying not to love Mamalee, see him now try harder
not to love me; I'm aware of how he tries, a middling effort,
not to prefer me in Ralls Janet's presence
over his wife with sunset-colored eyes,
the green obliterated. Sinking sun eyes).

All Adlers did some kind of spirit work, Sully said
but there were many kinds of spirits, and Mamalee
chided him for trying to link Rev. Adler to evil ones
for no reason other than the reverend's knowing Peter Perry
who was not actually any relation to the reverend;
for no reason than his not condemning slavery
from his pulpit

where he practiced the usual sermon while
Sully pounded usefulness and protection back
into the roof. "What does it matter, Sully?"
Mamalee asked the little man who loved her
but not secretly, but without guilt and shame,
who sometimes took her in his deformed arms;
"What does it matter?"
she repeated, "Rev. Adler doesn't keep any slaves.
He's nobody's master, not even his own. Ask him

and he'll tell you that *he* has a master, that *he*
is the Lord's slave. He's not important, Sully.
He's too weak to help. Only a weak man
has to hide behind the Lord so completely.
He says that slavery will end only when it's
the Lord's will. He never thinks

on how the Lord's will could be for somebody
to take action. Ask him how does he figure out
what is the Lord's will and what isn't. Ask him

and all he'll do is tell you that it's not the Lord's will
for him to know what is the Lord's will and what isn't
or he would know."

Reverend Moses Dunn out of Nashville
who came here for revival wouldn't have it.
Wouldn't be impressed with the angel bees.
He'd been stung, too,

and even though the stinging got him into preaching
he didn't praise or recommend it.

He called Irene Perry's bee hived mouth
the most ridiculous church he'd ever seen,
worse than in the uncivilized territories to the west
when he'd been, finding it too much trouble
to keep dust out of his Bible, so he was back for good,
on a narrower circuit.
Especially preaching in the mountains
with the echoes agreeing with and emphasizing every word.

He said you might as well call it miracle
when flies circle over carcasses
because in keeping to circles
the flies were acting out halos.
And the stink was just to make the miracle
conspicuous; if you had a nose you couldn't miss
such distinguished stinking.

And that meant any skunk was a prophet
of the church of the beehived mouth.

He was a preacher with as much a feel for life
as for heaven, and wouldn't stand for nonsense
in either one. Realistic, he was. Practical.
Not at all what Peter Perry usually liked.

Sully used to belong to Reverend Dunn
(who never married), cleaning up behind the horses
that Reverend Dunn brought right into the churches,
especially (of course) outdoor services
so that they would hear the preaching and be changed
into a Pegasus breed

even though there was never any sign of the change,
no transfigurating in the barn with bees making honey
in a horse neck or painting honey on horse teeth,
no reviving the dead with horse breath.

Traveling with Reverend Dunn
was how Sully had his legendary hundred children,
probably no more than six or seven, if that,
but he believed otherwise. So did Peter Perry,
the widened permissiveness of deformity.
I'd never seen any of them (as far as I knew)
but out of respect for Sully, I asked everyone
I met if they were a child of Sully.

Every time somebody told the story of Sully
especially when Sully told it himself
another child or two
was added on. It was as if Dwarf Sully was another Noah,
building something that would survive
the coming destruction
for which he was preparing
and getting a head start on replenishing the earth
with his own.

There were supposed to be a few little Dunns
across Kentucky, too. There'd be more than a few
if that story were told as much; it wasn't
Sully's favorite.

Sully had a master before Reverend Dunn,
up until Sully when he was just a child
grabbed hold of that master's gun
and twisted it around that master's neck
just as if gunmetal wasn't anything but a piece of rope

—believe if you want to, with Master Peter,
that Dwarf Sully charmed the gun, but even if you don't,
it was still built on the distorted truth of Sully catching
a whip in his teeth, and with his teeth, cracking the whip
and sending that master to the ground. Couldn't beat Sully.
The power, Peter Perry believed, of dwarfism.
The beating meant for Sully ended up
on whomever was trying to beat him.
He was protected by powers
no master could subdue

so that master, who was giving up his stony acres
and heading west where gold did the work of the sun,
sold Sully to Reverend Dunn for the price
of seeing the fear of God put in him,
though I don't believe that master has been paid yet.

Sully and Reverend Dunn were kind of friends
without trust; they liked each other fine enough
but shared no trust. Reverend Dunn preaching through
the country with a wise dwarf of Egypt on a horse
at his side. They had a near about perfect understanding
that was betrayed when Reverend Dunn
got to be good friends with Peter Perry
who took communion in the fields
and then Mamalee took it, too.
One bottle. One glass.

When Peter Perry's friendship with Reverend Dunn
was secure, the reverend traded his friend Sully
for a share of the corn crop after it became whiskey
and more communion. Peter Perry had to have
the dwarf. Would have sold his soul. The wagon loaded

up with bottles, Reverend Dunn drove down the roads
with the bottles making music banging into each other,
the joyful noise, Reverend Dunn said, of secular salvation.
He said that folk everywhere he went needed medicine.

Upon occasion, the bottles banged songs of escape
next to slave arms, legs, chests, necks also in the wagon.

Reverend was the man's name,
not his title. Folk assumed that since he was *Reverend*
that he was a real preacher, but Sully let on as to how
he never was. *Reverend* wasn't the name of his heart.
He was no closer to the Lord than anybody else was. If
he was a real preacher, he'd have to be Rev. Reverend Dunn,
just as Captain would have to be Cap. Captain

to take on title (but *name* is more than title
so isn't necessary for the man who is in command of his life
or for the man who saves himself already).

He insisted that Master Peter bury the beehive prophet.

And left right after explaining to Master Peter
why slaves endure "the splendid suffering
that the artifice of slavery is for. Heaven will regale
the triumph of their pain and will remove fully the scabs
they have worn over the entirety of their wounded skin.
Even you would agree, Brother Peter, that it will be a glorious sight
when the last scab is removed from the last Negro
who joins the rest of the healed in a stupefying marvel

that during all that time slaving,
his white skin was busy healing under a scab so big
he himself mistakenly thought the scab was his skin."

It amused me to hear that some white skin
was healing under my teabark.
I'm not worried about any such disaster as that.
Some slaves were whiter looking than Reverend Dunn; what
healing was taking place there? What about Albino Pearl?

Reverend Dunn looked like a piece of mountain come to life
and he preached from any book, believing that all books,
like everything else, had obtained the Lord's approval to exist
or they wouldn't. According to Reverend Dunn, every word
was God's word, even the foul words which he said were
necessary so the Lord could punish the evil as he couldn't do
with just a dictionary of sorghum.

"Let those who disagree be damned," he said.

That means he'd preach from my book.

THE HARVESTING OF MYSTERIOUS WAYS

Master Peter could be close up on you sometimes.
Studying, working his experiments.
Or he sent Bishop Adler, sometimes, to check up
on you, observe your activities,
make sure you were working as hard as Bishop
was supposed to be working the row beside you,
master in training, lover of tradition;

Bishop Adler who was still something of a child
as far as I could see, not much older than me,
Master Peter's nephew from Knoxville to help
sometimes with planting and harvesting, though I heard
him say that he was being educated beyond doing
hard work anymore, so he could just run
the Adler whiskey business.
He was talking to himself; wouldn't hardly
have been talking to me. He liked his distance
from his inferior-minded uncle.

Sometimes Peter Perry was so close up on you
you didn't know whose breathing was whose.

Close enough to read these words through my dress.
close enough to want to read them, maybe write some
of his own. Not that I can have anything that's
not also his. My private cocoon
and I have let him in by writing about him so much,
making him the center of my thoughts.

As if I love him
but I do not.

So close up on you as if he was a white shadow,
As if your black shadow had had all the black
scared out of it.
White bear after my honey, after my teabark—
I'm all delicious.

I didn't hear the shadow coming, didn't feel it
but it was here, with me.
Bishop summoned it, an accident of his getting closer
to me than Peter Perry wanted. So Peter Perry came
to intervene, claim his private stock of honey teabark
from a nephew who would never understand
subtle control and punishment. The art of denial.

I had been stripped down to the *Varl* in me

but he didn't see the *Varl*, couldn't see through black
—unless it was full of holes
—unless like the night sky, it was full of holes
where the *Varl* in it was trying to break free.

Checking up on me. Close up on me. If anything
in the field was as tall as uncle, tall as nephew,
it would be marked for harvest and cut down.

Full moon midnight mysterious harvesting
of words for my quilt-cocoon. That was what
I was all about doing. Largest full-faced moon
I'd ever seen, enlarging so I could see better
to stitch better thoughts (though they were
about him. An infatuation, an infestation
in my mind. What's going on with the *Varl* in me,
the *Varl* Master Peter put in me?
Struggle between Dob and Master
Peter for dominance in my mind. I love Dob,
thinking about getting even more strategic

with my cocoon, building it up where
a baby would build me up, Dob's baby
as Peter Perry enraged would think, Master Peter's baby
as Dob would think until I'd tell him. Would tell him
quickly: My own baby, as I would know, birth
of free me breaking the cocoon.
I don't want Master Peter to know this, how
occupied I am with him. Clandestine, twisted
love letters of a sort, and wearing them all over me
as his substitute. I don't want him to know the Varl
under the Varl he sees, the internal Varl the cocoon
protects. I have to have some of me for me alone,
even loving Dob, some of me is mine alone; some
of me loves me. But so much Peter Perry in this book,
as if it's his book. Can't keep him out of it. Need
to keep him out of it.)

Close, so close up on me

while I was taking moonlight liberty
lost in it
sitting on the Jimbo tree stump needle-writing
when

this time, he was too
close up on me.

   —Bishop breath close—
   —Peter Perry breath closer—

Bishop told Peter Perry I was up to something.
Bishop out midnight smoking in the Jimbo clearing
in the slave part of the woods, thinking of his needs.
I didn't see or hear him. I was already caught
by what I was doing. Couldn't see or hear anything
but how sure I was that I needed to do what I was doing,

how sure I was of the secret. I took on being completely
Free too soon. Believed the cocoon was working.
Believed Varl had powers.

Master Peter reading over my shoulder
as fast as I write-stitch something.
Dob thoughts. Thoughts of Perry treason.
How I knew the master loved me and would love me
even more for being now more strange, more valuable,
loved me more than anything.

"Want me to sign that for you?"
he asked. "You're putting words in my mouth, so
I may as well write them, too. You really think
I could love *you* that way?" he said, loving me
that way.

I knew he did. And he was loving this encounter.
He was supposed to punish me. For Bishop's benefit
he had to hit me, for his own he had to make contact
with my skin. Loving me didn't mean
he couldn't hurt me.

What could I say? Deny that I was writing
with needle and thread? Tell him I was making him
a shirt? Adorning it with Bible verses,
following orders from his wife?
What could I do, except accept the consequences
of being caught? Didn't I realize
just this possibility?
Didn't I want Ralls Janet to see the garment
I had sewn for myself, one of a kind, the most
precise tailoring? Most perfect fit?

Bishop was finally enjoying being here.

"Get on back to the house, Bishop."
He didn't move.

Crickets. Owls. Whippoorwills.

Night air.

I should have been with Dob.

"These are free papers I'm making.
That doesn't surprise you, does it . . . Master (whispered)
Peter?"

"Those can't be free papers; you don't have any paper."

"It doesn't mean anything . . . Sir (whispered)."

"Everything means something, Varl.
Aren't you smart enough to know that?
You being able to do this, to think of sewing
your words—that's not natural; it means something.
I wonder what you've written on the back side of
my shirts? I'll read them by lamplight.
And us being in the woods tonight—means something.
I stand above you; you sit on a stump, master
and slave. But what else? It's an equation.
We are variables. You have this talent
that can't be explained. Yet you are beneath me.
This talent that is my talent because you're mine.
This is an equation, a riddle. Are you smart enough
to solve it?"

"Somebody might hear you, Peter Perry.
Someone who won't like the way you're speaking to me,
someone who won't understand that none
of the slave/master rules has been broken.

Don't all masters love what they do
however they choose to do it?"

He dared to smile at me; so, so pleased.

"The way you speak, know things. It's not right,
Varl. I want to understand it . . . You put *slave* first;
the *slave*/master rules."

I looked at him and he dared to smile at me again.

"Ralls Janet might shoot you."

"Never."

"Her family makes guns."

"Never."

"Well, then Mamalee."

"She might shoot a white man, but not me.
We have an . . . agreement."

"And now you want one with me?"

"Not quite."

He stooped. Slight sour mash on his breath.
His tongue fermenting.

"What do you do with these cloth pages, Varl?
I'm assuming this is not the first one; you're
too confident sitting there, the needle sparkling.
Should this have gone to some new curtains,
tablecloths, sheets, new clothes for my wife

and daughter? Are you stealing from their
future wardrobe? How are you going to pay me
for what you've taken?"

I didn't say anything.

"It's the principle, Varl. It's appearance
that's at stake. You *are* my slave.
Why can't you understand that?
How can you not know what that means?
What's so fascinatingly wrong
with you?"

Everything that was wrong with me
made me right for him.

Scared, so scared now.
Peter Perry has powers.

Wanting Dob. King Dob
is right for me.

Master Peter touched my back and felt
too much thickness.
He pulled my dress away
from the back of my neck and felt for
the source of thickness.

"You're clever, Varl. Frighteningly clever.
But go ahead and tell me anyway what you do,"
he patted the thickness, "with all those pages.
I might want to read them. Maybe I'll visit
the Varl library."

He plans to read the Master's book
of flesh

and would not plan to had I not read his books,
proving there were things about me that to know
he'd have to uncover.
More things now than before.

I think I should call Mamalee but I don't rush
to call on outside myself. A scream would hurt
the niceness of night
before it has to be hurt
so to his remark I give nothing; I treat his threat
as not being real
as the idle close warmth of him.

"Aren't you going to call Mamalee?"

He wants proof he understands me, is so much a master
he can predict, but to make him right
would make me less rare
and would lower me
to ordinary danger, ordinary pleasure
of a master who doesn't need to use words.

"Call her, Varl."

He touches me with only his voice. Breath
on my face, thin damp fingers. My ears funnel
his *varl* in me.

"No reason to. Nothing's happening but night noises
and things that depend on the dark getting their chance.
Lots of small things enlarge in opportunity to."

"But you are not a small thing."

"Not anymore. And you are not getting your chance,"
I say too bold

for him to give up and lower me
as he would have if I'd called Mamalee.

Instead, his smile rushes sunrise
as I become the most valuable thing he has
for being from now on
the most difficult to keep

same as I was when all of me could be bought.
Now he wants to steal the rest
knowing it is not his no matter what he says

but I am the better thief,
to be taking even more from him, his own will
to resist. I can keep him occupied for all nights, fill
what can't get full in him long enough to pour it out
like moonlight turning water when I say *turn*
drying up when I say *dry*

as he tries to get closer and closer to what I pull
further and further away from him with every stitch.

He is too encouraged.
I sit tall as I can but do not seem to rise
taller though the shadow of him is a lengthening tower
overtaking mine easily like scent taking over a room

inviting me to first breath of dogwood.
My nose clogged with sour dogwood in him seeping out
Nothing to breathe but what he breathes. Turn
my head, and cheek, ear, or nose would touch him, shift
any way at all and touch him. So don't move
and seem to wait for him. Can't get past him
without touching—it seems his night air will prosper
into dawn until prosperity sticks in my throat,
so "Mamalee!" I yell. "Mamalee!"

and the word pushes it out

and she stopped the sun from rising all the way.
She came to me. Nothing else
would come so quickly, would break rules
so fast. It was Mamalee. Coming. Closer, closer,
closer than him.

The darkness that was already there
had to be her. Now it took on her shape
because I needed it to.

"Mamalee, Master Peter's real impressed with me.
I work so well, do what I do so fine,
he can't believe it's the work of an ordinary slave.
Bishop told him about it!
and he had to see for himself

my working through the midnight. Making him . . . a shirt
touched with moonlight, cloth rubbed on with moonlight.

Mamalee! A shirt is all that's happening;
a master shirt. A rich shirt."

Even she didn't know that I was so wrapped up
in things like this.

"Go on home, Varl." Mamalee told me.

"Stay, Girl. Your work's not done. I can't believe
you'd think your work was done."

My mama, my master
couldn't agree,
were not supposed to agree

because *mama* and *master* were opposites.

I stayed by Mamalee. She was the darkness
but I was the reason for it. I would be the cause
of anything that happened
to her. I stayed to get an opposite story to tell
from the one he would tell. He couldn't see
all of what I could see. I couldn't see
all of what he could see.

I heard something and turned my head
to see Bishop spitting seeds.
Spitting out also my boldness that made him sick
with anger. He had swallowed as much of it
as Peter Perry.
He wasn't as big as Dob,
not as nice to look at.
So I didn't look anymore. This was the last time
I was ever going to look at him

so I wouldn't have to read him better
so when I saw him in my mind, he'd be
spitting seeds of my boldness, planting them
for me to harvest. That was the look
my picture of him froze into. Spitting seeds

and thinking about going back next week
to Knoxville, courting somebody there, somebody
Sully said was black way back where it didn't show.
Not a ruffle in her hair, not a twist or knot
even when it was so hot my hair puffed and shriveled.
My Living Cotton Head, Peter Perry said
first time he saw it. Couldn't do anything
that didn't delight him. Everything I did
spoke lovingly to him of oddity
but all I did was exist, be myself,

try to exercise a right that I hadn't meant
to include him.
I should be in the north, Pennsylvania, Michigan,
New York, where I would not be oddity, other
escaped slaves writing books. I want to run, but
haven't yet. Dob would, taking
one of the master's guns with him. The moment
that I'm ready. I must like in some part
being exceptional
here. I really must be something of an oddity.

Tonight I made it storm.

When it rained
her hair slicked down as if she'd just been born,
that girl black way back where it didn't show
so couldn't be oddity.

I can't say her name so it won't look as if
I might know what I'm talking about,
it's just something I heard
the same as I heard birds and didn't know what
they were saying. I have to be an interpreter
of what birds say. What flowing water says.

Protect her. Couldn't protect Jessper.
Need now to protect myself

Earlier I told Lusa what the rain said,
the same thing that the rain said every time, and she
couldn't find game in it when I told her the rain said:
Varl has powers, Varl has powers, so she went running
to her mistress mama telling her that *Varl has powers,*
that I could make the rain talk; she heard it say
that *Varl has powers;* she heard me teach it to say that

and saw me make it rain from a cloud that formed
just over her head when I snapped out a tablecloth
so I could fold it. It didn't rain anywhere else.
Then that tablecloth disappeared just as a cloud
does disappear when it gets all its rain out.
Folds itself
smaller and smaller to nothing.

"I'm just sweeping, Ra—*Mistress*" (I'm almost laughing)
"Ralls Janet. Dirt must be flying up in Lusa's—*Miss* Lusa's—ears
because I'm sweeping so well
just for you. Dirt's playing a trick on her.
Dirt shouldn't do that but dirt's dirt; what else
can you expect from dirt?

Maybe she could keep her ears covered.
I'll make something to protect her ears—and
her eyes, nose, and mouth too now that I think about it,
because they're all in danger when I'm sweeping

so very well

as I usually sweep for you. Won't any dirt
flying up from a broom I'm using bother her
anymore."

That's what I said.

But I couldn't talk like that right then. My tongue
was trembling, probably bruising itself from hitting
so much, even though it was lightly hitting, up against
my teeth. Couldn't keep my thoughts anywhere but here,
they left and came right back, *right back*
as if ordered to. Thoughts close up on me,
Peter Perry close up on me: two masters now.

I moved closer to Mamalee as if
I was trying to blend into her
even though I wanted to stay me no matter what
happened. She didn't need
for me to be her
in order for her to be her. We were just close
like this so the rest of danger couldn't get in.
We were blocking it.
We had no gap, no place where what we were together
was weak.

An unnatural fortress. Bishop spitting seeds to knock it down.

What did this look like to them? What did Master Peter
and Bishop really see? Power didn't budge
when Mamalee got here but air changed,
dropped all dogwood.
She affected them faster than anything
other than me. But they were still the masters.
What were they thinking? What were they feeling?
Could Peter Perry make sense of so many contradictions?

—when he was close
up on me—when he moved away

to the same distance between him and Mamalee
as the distance between me and him.

Has to hit me, touching already his objective, has
to shift it, hit me, the appearance in front of Bishop

who has seen too much.

Was Bishop waiting to lunge so he could hold first me
then Mamalee down while Master Peter punished the other?

Should I uncover my back, one of the best, like plum skin
with no purple,
and remind him with moonlight reflecting off its smoothness
that he didn't want to ruin it? Or would he think
I was showing off or inviting him to things I don't even
fully invite my own thoughts to yet?

What did they really think?
Did they really feel?

Close to me
without knowing the me they were close to,
As if they were really far away.

Master Peter wanting to know the me
he was close to, but why? What would it
do for him to know me? He knew enough.

Then anger
came close, too.

That palpable kind that Sully
could get careless with. Maybe I could, too.
I had already said too much, revealed too much.
Maybe I could speak some more and try to fix
things. Maybe in this light
he could listen to my reason.
Maybe if I didn't look at him
he'd be persuaded. He was Perry; he wasn't
Jessper's Staley.

They know we're people. They have to know that
even if they disregard that knowing. I am not
an oddity. Being literate
doesn't make me an oddity. No freak of nature.

No deformity.
Nothing makes sense but that they know it, as human
as themselves, yet act against their own knowing.

That's what was deformed.

They have to know.
Peter Perry has to know all the time, not
just when Bishop wasn't around. Needs to admit
what he knows about me when it's not convenient.
Then more of the bold he loves in me so much
would be his own.

Even Bishop has to know we die, we eat, we fight, we hurt, grieve,
we bleed, defend ourselves, dream, we run away, we want
to be free. He has seen it tonight. I am his teacher. All slaves
teach this; all masters know

but maybe Peter Perry has forgotten, because it is convenient;
maybe I should remind him, because that is convenient for me.
But even if I didn't, he had to know and Bishop had to know
we didn't plan to keep it like this forever.
Oh soon. Soon.
We planned to be as free as them, freer
than them because they were not so free that they
could stop

coming close
up on me,

watching me, keeping me a slave. Breaking
my concentrating on the *varl*. They knew
I was looking for the end.
They knew

I didn't think the slave life was enough life.
They knew I knew
there was something else.
They knew I knew them.

A nightbird call eased the tension.
Its sound spit into the dark air.

"Varl your youngest child, Leticia?"

"Yes, Sir. You know that."

"How many others have you got?"

"None that's alive."

"How are you tolerating that?"

"Like I have to. They lived as best
they could, both of my dead sons over
in Murfreesboro. They had jobs, Master Peter."

She whispered the *master*; it was barely audible.
He liked the sound of the deep wind acknowledging him
as a master.
He liked Mamalee giving him the deep subdued wind.
I could tell he liked it, the way he leaned, rubbed
his hands together
as if he was fixing to ask Mamalee to dance
but was a little intimidated and shy because
of how important and beautiful her rudeness was.
And he had to get by her to get to me. More
beautiful. So intimidating he'd sell his soul.
She didn't loosen though.

"They could make things, fix things.
Made sails, fixed sails in Baltimore
and was doing that till Captain . . . disappeared
and they were sent back to Tennessee.
They were having lives same as what
you dream of having. They were
living out some of *your* dreams."

     I do that for him, too.

"I sent for them, remember, Mamalee?
I thought you'd want your sons.
You might not have more . . . with Captain—that's what
you'd want me to call Odysseus, isn't it?
—And what do you want me to call Varl?"

     He looked at me to ask that because
     he wanted to call me out from those things holding me
     from him; he knew he could hold me better, one way
     when Bishop looked, another way
     when Bishop didn't.

"Leave Varl alone, Peter. You said you would.
When she was born you said it.
And it doesn't matter what you called Varl's father.
What he called himself is more important. Tells
a lot more about him than anything else.
You know, I had so much
with Captain that I don't likely need more;
don't know where
I'd put it, all that wonderful extra, but you're right.
Having more with Captain is one of those unlikely things.

Yet and still I'm not going to say what can't
ever happen. I have heard of mysterious ways
and I have seen mysterious lights in the sky.

I didn't know what they were
and nobody could tell me anything
but that the lights were there."

"You scared of that? I know Varl's not, but you?"

> I am beside and between what I am beside, my master
> and my mama really talking about what is to be done
> about me. I am rising above her, soon to be over
> his head as his personal dark cloud making weather
> just for him, Mamalee having to say that *it looks like rain*
> though she won't be the one getting wet.
> I am beside and between her fear as it grows
> big enough to seem a strong thing on its own, no longer
> afraid of being fear.

"No. I took it as Captain signaling to me
from a lighthouse up in heaven.
Besides, you are somewhat of a mystery, too,
and I'm not scared of you."

"Maybe I should do something about that."

"I can't advise you on that.
You have your own mind, but you might want
to think about how you'll feel if you don't succeed
in making me scared. What will you do then?"

"Concerned about me, are you? I'm glad
you care. There's not many like you, *Leticia*."

"I believe you're right."

"And not many like me
who would not only let a slave insult him,

but enjoy it, too. The insult doesn't
change any of our circumstances."

"I'm glad you're not bothered by the truth.
I'm not bothered by anything when Varl or *Free*
is at stake."

He was fixing to smile but then didn't
let the smile happen. His smile was only for me.
He gave Mamalee what he wanted her to have.

"Varl isn't scared of me,
and I know just what to do with her."

The smile came out in my direction. Bishop took it
for a match, one of his uncle's Lucifers
from England that I have handled for him, balancing flame,
and Bishop started to burn. Fire has much longer arms
than a man. Quicker body in every way
and would soon be close up on me thicker than dogwood
mashed and sour in my throat.

"Peter Perry, it was love that brought my sons back.
What loves *you* so much it would return to you after
it gets the success of getting away from you?
My sons came back. They're dead now,
buried in Murfreesboro, but even before that, *you*

didn't own them
and hadn't owned then for a while. Not really.

Came back, and you tried
to put free-minded men up for sale,
and they bought each other;
you hadn't figured on them having the money
and buying each other

and their cleverness got them killed. Somebody
didn't like their cleverness.
Do you recollect who it was who didn't like
their cleverness?"

"Memory fails me, Leticia. I adore cleverness, myself."

Clever, clever dogwood night.

"Are you surprised that something would fail you?"

He looked at her hard.

"*Sir*," she added quietly.

Bishop Adler was still spitting
but the seeds were burning and spreading fire
on what they hit.
The "sir" came out just in time with what he spit.
It was as if the "sir" was spit, too.

—What loves him so much it would come back?
—What loves him so much it wouldn't leave him?
Ralls Janet still here. Mamalee still here.
Varl right here.
Bishop rubbing his thighs, getting ready,
friction fire.

"Master Peter," I say, the *master* tasting funny
because I don't say it this way, as if I mean it,
as if the word is burning me. "Master Peter,"
I say thinking I sound subdued

but I don't. "THAT'S ENOUGH OF THAT." The fire
of a Bishop was talking. "UNCLE PETER—"

"—I didn't kill your sons. I wasn't in Murfreesboro . . .
at the time. And I'm going to say again that
I have long been an admirer of cleverness
when I found it where it didn't belong.
Devil's not what we think.
He was awfully clever up in heaven."

"I didn't say my sons were killed in Murfreesboro, Sir;
I said they were *buried* there."

The fire was walking. "UNCLE PETER—"

"Master Peter—" I say, inviting him to look at me
toward the fire just over my shoulder. Then I can't say more;
hot Bishop rage is too close. Mamalee hadn't noticed
because she had stopped being slave in this confrontation
in which she thought she was the fire that was there.

"I'll tell you this too, Sir.
You might not have killed them
but I know you know who did.
All of you know who has killed a black man.
You know because knowing
is your tavern brag. But it's what

you don't know that should be your concern.
And a big part of what you don't know is what I know.

Does my cleverness offend you, too,
down here below heaven?"

"Mamalee," I yell, sitting on the ground
tall as campfire. "I'm burning up."

But so is she.

"You're not for sale."

And so is Peter Perry.

"What does that have to do with cleverness
being offensive?"

"Reminds you what you don't like to know
about who you are. Besides, I can't get
a good enough price for it
or for whatever package the cleverness comes in."

"Mamalee," I yell again, noticing cleverness burning
brightest of all. Each one of us clever in what we were doing.

"Why not, Sir?"

"You're good for more than your work; you're good
for conversation. Nobody would pay me
what the conversation is worth. For a moment with you
like this one."

But he was looking at me now. The moment with her
was with me also. Now
he saw the troubling fire of Bishop. Now he saw
his own cleverness become smoke. Flying smoke.

"—Bishop!" Peter Perry said like a master
and I felt free, a foot on my hem where I sat with dress
spread in small circle of defense, lifted.

"I beg your pardon, Sir, but this is not a conversation,
this is prosecution and defense. And if you want conversation
you could talk to your wife or just to the walls
if not to your favorite horse."

"Same thing, isn't it? And my favorite horse would be
Varl now." He said and doused more of the flames.
"Are you giving *me* orders now, Leticia?"

"I prefer that you call me *Mamalee*, Sir, just
as everyone else does."

"Of course you do, but I don't have to call you anything at all.
Varl," he said, calling me something, "grew up quite well, better
than you know. Definitely your best crop."

The fire was only in Bishop's eyes now; finally, he could enjoy
the look of things, look of me, now, properly thing again.

"Sir, what do you know about how she grew? You promised.
She's not like that corn," Mamalee said, her arms spread wide
as if she was trying to hold back crows.

"Well, yes she is, Mamalee; she's just like that corn.
It's mine. She's mine. Everything you see is mine.
Leticia—You do have something, though, my name.
YOU'RE A *PERRY* SLAVE.
Leticia Perry—that's like a badge.
Keep it shiny. . . Mamalee."

She moved to strike him. "Mamalee!" I yelled on fire
to stop her, lunging to stop her from striking him
as she wanted, as Bishop wanted—blows, lashes
as he moved with me, eager, so I kept moving

because if I were to be Free, I needed
more room; I couldn't be free where I was standing
because free wouldn't fit in such a tight,
breathless place

111

where Free would have to die. I kept moving

into a perfect position, perfect justification for Mister Bishop
who spit some more seeds of mysterious ways
right by my feet

to grab me. It sounded like someone shot a gun into the air
or was it a cannon of voices become too hot and explosive?

      Dob shooting from the trees? .
      Of course, Dob? Gunless Dob?

      Tense quiet now.

Mamalee was close up on me again, close hug. Then Sully
was close up on her close up on me. Hoe in hand.

"You not going to touch her, Sir."

"You're not going to touch her, Sir."

"You're not going to touch me, Sir."

Three voices, three walls standing
against fourth wall made from bricks
quickly taken from Bishop's hot stove of disapproval
so that Peter could have something to stand up with.

Standing
though it wasn't his way to touch his slaves,
not his way to go past threats,
not his way *yet*.

His way wasn't even to put that *yet* there
until tonight for me. Now I had to worry, fear changes,
had to pray against change
ever happening,

had to pray he stayed the way he is. He is
your master.

And he loves me.
I'm afraid of how much he loves me.
How much he showed me tonight that he loves me.
The way he loves me with fear.
He didn't touch me.

Bishop disgusted. Bishop ashamed
of his uncle. Bishop cursing. Bishop leaving
this nightmare in the morning. Bishop stomping
rage all the way to the house, yelling to Ralls Janet
to get out of his way. Ralls Janet
who had been watching the darkness,

her own flame, her own slender candle of self put out.
Slender candle shaped in the dark distance
like gun.

I didn't know where Dob was. If it was a gun
it wasn't Dob's gun. Why didn't he protect me?

My Dob.
My Mamalee.
My master

whose smile next day blended into my morning
like an apology that I accepted but didn't trust

not to turn away from its own definition,
Peter Perry only Peter if he gets to be alone with that

and close up on nothing else.

SLAUGHTER AND THE VARL IN ME

"Which one is the hog,"
Peter Perry laughed
as he watched Sully prepare
to butcher one.

Future business associates
were coming; the meat
would be fresh-kill
of a favorite.

He might get to own a share
of a major cotton gin and textile mill
near Knoxville to complement his other holdings.
Farmed more for fun now than for necessity.
And he might have an opportunity to become rather
profitably involved with tobacco.

Wants to impress them.
Ralls Janet to smell good.
Silk chemise under silk.
Lusa to be practicing her letters,
making words like *Duke*.
Wants me to serve, the cloth books
to remain in great places on me.

He has already taken over nearby land
of failed farms and displaced Indians.

An enterprising man.

The *Great Book of Insectean Marvels*
left out. Its superb plates. His collection
out, too, where the associates will take

Adler whiskey. Some talk of that new
Darwin stuff—to prove he knows it, and what
an effect it'll have on understanding all
the oddity in the room.
Then Peter Perry lectures on his latest acquisitions
while I serve them drinks, say a word or two
in other languages that do not exist,
Varl a corruption of *marvelous* in that tongue,
biggest prize of his collection.
Dwarf Sully will shine their shoes
and tend their horses. Leased slaves will assist.
Mamalee will cook from unknown recipes
that won't remain unknown, but the taste
is worth the loss, the knowledge better
than mystery; whiskeyed biscuits.

Some of Ralls Janet's
silent showy flowers for the table.
Cut blooms.

Pearl will show them to the room
where they will spend the night,
birth of the Hotel Perry where Chickasaw
used to live. Pearl white as a pearl,
parchment Pearl, her face written on
with blue veins of the boundaries of
Perry property.
Albino Pearl shows them the way.

"Goad the hog first, Sully; then kill it,"
Master Peter instructed, directing his experiment

to make the hog a fighter to get that bold flavor
in the flesh before the killing and the gutting.
You might want to taste bold
for its deeper taste than all meek meat.

You might want to sleep with bold
for its deeper pleasure than all meek meat.

Varl bold to be watching
Sully with the hog.

After a couple hours of provoking it
the animal had all the meanness
and resistance beaten out,
supplying a tender layer, softened layer
all of fat that would melt around the cooking meat
as salve and balm, mercy and forgiveness

for the killer. It was forgiveness
that tastes so good. Your absolution; meat
wants this. When Mamalee cooked it
and it tasted divine, there seemed to be
double forgiveness:
meat forgiving how it was treated, Mamalee
forgiving how she was treated. Forgiveness—
the master wanted it, thought he was getting it
in the form of the forced cooperation
of what got mistreated.

So pure the whole mess became after that cooperation
and forgiveness, that in a skillet, the blood ran clear
out of the pork, clearer than the creek.
Standing there, tending it
so that it didn't burn, Mamalee didn't speak,
handed a silent spoonful over to Ralls Janet
so she could taste broth and gravy right after Mamalee.
Same spoon.

Sometimes I think there is no
other water
than the clearness out of pork.

So transparent.

Hiding nothing.

Obvious what had to happen
for the clearness to be present.

Clearness of my name.
Varl or Free.

Clear no matter what fresh laws
come about to halt any black progress.

It's clear that I am breaking laws
including laws of nature as interpreted
by some men.

I am *Free*
and I am Varl.
Free most of my life,
Varl longer, all my life.

Before I could even talk, I would come to Mamalee
when she called "Varl."

That's the word that made me notice something
other than what I was noticing.
That's the word that got my attention.
And I got used to it. I made *Varl* mean me
more than it ever meant a horse.
I was Free when I did that.

When Master Peter called his horse "Varl,"
that name was for him to know one horse from another
and that was all. He wasn't opening a door with *Varl*
but I do. And behind that door I distinguished myself
from everything else.

If I called a tree *Varl* or called a bite of honeycake *Varl*
it was because I was recognizing some *Varl* in it, some *me* in it.

So even though I'm really Free
I can't throw *Varl* away. I have made *Varl* mean more
than Master Peter intended. It's not just a word; *Varl*
is me. My secret. Both sides
of the cocoon. Master Peter doesn't mean *me*

when he says *Varl*, he doesn't know the *me* in *Varl*;
he didn't think there was a me to put in Varl
beyond the me he made of me,
he didn't think *Varl* was something anything could be
put in but a horse race.

Now that I seemed to have blossomed
into something more right before his eyes,
he still didn't mean the fullness of the blossoming
when he said *Varl*, when he wanted some of Varl's petals
in his buttonhole.

The blossoming he was aware of was as ephemeral
as that of any other flower;
he didn't take petals to be botanical wings
the beauty brief, effects everlasting.

Pray for him
because he can't admit the deviancy
of his love for me. Something is wrong
with him.

If only Ralls Janet could understand
that something was more wrong with him
than was wrong with her.

I know he loves me.
I know there are no limits now
to what love will allow.
He is lost in loving me.

———

Ever since I understood I was a slave
I wanted to be free. Some of *Varl*
means that wanting.

And I am Free now, your freedom doesn't come to you
because of your location; you have to feel it inside
or you'd just be a slave in a free place. Lost.
Inside my cocoon I am already Free.

Inside my cocoon
I'm extending Varl's definition to include *Free*.

Mamalee called me Varl last night.
And also called me Free.

Though having been a slave, I'm not sure
if it was possible to be completely free. Possible
to purge all evidence of my enslavement. As if
it had never happened. It did happen. I don't want
any part of Varl's life diminished. I don't want
any part of Varl's life denied.
My slave life isn't anything
to be ashamed of. I claim it. My slave life
is my life. My slave life is a serious matter.

I won't throw it away even though I'm Free.
Varl's slave life is part of the Free life.

Whether or not Free is what I thought
it was, I want it; I put it on
whether or not something else,
like *Varl*, the well-loved *Varl*,

might be more comfortable sometimes,
certainly something else sometimes might be easier.
No matter what it is, I want it; bear-
headed, possum-footed, deer-hearted, duck-legged
—no matter that there's no human in it at all,
I want the free, the free

that I see in field mice that get to wear wheat for fur
and get lifted up
to where field mice couldn't get on their own,
lifted up by hawk, I know, hungry hawk, but lifted
and gets to see
just before giving up its life to feed the hawk,
a sight of the world, shape of the field it had never
even realized was the fact of its home.
It sees a truth that nobody
could have told it. So, yes, hurry up

to when it's more Free than Varl.
This new language, ability to translate
what has crows saying *Free* all morning
having found something more beautiful than they are.

'Bout ready to burst
from the cocoon.

BURN

"Varl, you're going to have to be more careful
coming to see me. Master Staley has taken
to taming slaves for a fee, capturing runaways
for a bounty. He would have no trouble at all
taking you as a runaway caught early in her escape.
His farm is to the north of Master Perry's,
right along your route."

"Look." Her neck and face were burned.

"Why'd he do this to you?
You can't stay there, Jessper.
What did you do to him?"

"I didn't fold the sheets right. Mistress Eveline
is confined to the bed and she doesn't see a human
face except for mine, only knows kindness from me
when I lift up the body she can't move and help her
take some tea down. Master Staley doesn't
want her. He wants me, Varl."

"You should run."

"He would find me."

"He would replace you.
You don't really think it matters to him
which slave he beds with?"

"He can't afford to replace me.
So he'd have to hunt me and punish me well
then bed with me on the same night.
Maybe that's why Mistress Eveline hates me

so much, knowing her husband isn't
going to give up those physical things
just because of her. I don't know, Varl.
I'm just so scared."

"You weren't too scared to come here tonight."

"I came *because* I'm scared.
I rather be caught here than anywhere.
Slaves don't get burned here."

"Not like your burn."

"Doesn't happen here. Not your body.
You might get your feelings burned,
but that's better. Better
if it's just pride that's nothing but ashes."

"Might be better in one way of thinking,
but still not good enough."

"I'm so scared—"

"—Wait, Jessper. I hear something."

I ran toward what I thought was moving
in the trees and bushes.

"Evening, Varl."

I gasped, fearing it had been Theodore Staley.

"Evening, Master Peter." I seemed relieved
to see him. He seemed pleased seeing himself
as my relief.

"Go on back to Jessper; I'm not going to spoil anything
tonight." I thought he might have tipped his hat
had he been wearing one. "Might buy her.
Might be taking over that whole farm."

Keeping my eyes on the stand of trees
I walked backwards to Jessper
and the Jimbo tree stump where I was caught before
needle-writing
Dob-kissing
Dob-kissing
Dob-kissing
(three times)

where Master Peter has learned he can find me
where I keep going as if I want him to find me
to know I do things that exclude him

for as long as possible
till he arrives. Relieved
to be no longer hiding.

"What is it, Varl?"

"Master Peter. Just Master Peter
keeping an eye on his property.
Letting that eye become other things
in his imagination."

Jessper stared at me. She'd never heard me
sound so sad. She'd never seen me seem
so vulnerable, seem so close to defeat, nearly burned.

"It's still better here," Jessper insisted.
"Why doesn't Sully protect you? Or Dob?"

I didn't have an answer for that.

"My brothers tried to protect me, Mamalee,
themselves. They're dead and buried now."

"Eveline had me burn myself. She couldn't do it
and of course she wouldn't invite her husband
to touch me in any way, even to burn me.
In case he liked it.—She only knew kindness
from me!—yet I didn't fold the sheets
to her liking, didn't iron them smooth enough
so that it would look like they weren't flawed,
didn't have bug-holes eaten out the corners.
She ordered me to take the hot smoothing iron
and hold it to the side of my face and neck."

"Oh, Jessper." I hugged her, hugged her, hugged her.
"She's paralyzed, Jessper—why would you obey her?
What could she do to you if you disobeyed? Oh, Jessper."

"I don't know."

Silence.

"Oh, Jessper. Go to Pearl. She'll put something
on this. Make it heal better."

"I don't want it to heal better
and I don't want to start a habit
of disobedience. Maybe I wouldn't be able
to resist disobedience when there was the most
danger in disobedience. I just don't want
to get accustomed to defiance.
I want this burn to be what a burn should be.
I don't want it soothed. This can't be
made better."

Silence. Master Perry holding his breath.
Mine, too.

"Varl, you wouldn't last long
if you belonged to someone else.
The way you talk to your master,
just the way you look at him—
you'd be dead."

"You burned yourself, Jessper.
YOU BURNED YOURSELF!"

"Please stop saying that."

She kept her hand on the side of her face and neck
as if it was the iron, as if she could never put it down.

I pried it loose.
Sat there with her quiet
so it could cool down.

No marks on me.

Outline of a confusion
of flattened roses on her face.

Of course Master Peter might want to buy her.

"Varl."

It was Dob.

"Jessper's been burned," I tell him,
reason to run to him, forgetting Peter Perry
might still be watching; don't want him to see me

with Dob so much. He might send Dob away.
Jealous like his wife. Me at the center
of both jealousies.

Dob turned to stone, stone grip
on his knife.

"I'll be fine," Jessper lies.
"Just touched my face with it; didn't
hold it there. Fastest touch
there's ever been. Mercy
that wouldn't have been there had the touch
come from a Staley hand."

"But, Jessper..."

What do we do? Cocoon and knife
as weapons. What do we do?
What good for her to spit in his food
when he was going to spit in her mouth?

Pearl will get some poison to her. And she'll feed him
a little bit everyday. Just to get him weak.
Just so he'll have to crawl to get to her
and she'll have time to take one more step backward,
delaying him till he collapses.
—I hear something.

"Get on home, Jessper. I'll see you
as soon as I can. I'm sorry I can't act
right now, and I don't know what I can
really do for you if you won't run.
Maybe I'll think of something."

"You're always thinking."

"I have to think. Don't want to lose my mind
to this. It swallows you. Then you can't think
of what lies beyond. I *will* think of something."
Don't want to mention Pearl or poison.
—I hear something.

"May not be much of anything beyond."

"Yes there is. I've been there. I write about
what I see and feel there. When I'm with Dob
I'm there."

"I wish Eveline Staley would be sorry.
I wish Theodore Staley would be sorry,"
Jessper said as she went home.
The something I heard seemed to follow her.
Fallen limb said *Jessper* when it broke under foot.

Me and Dob now.
Me and Dob not speaking.

His hand on my shoulder.
His hand on my waist.
I don't feel enough his hand on my shoulder.
I don't feel enough his hand on my waist

through the thickness of my cocoon.

Quiet.
Me and Dob quiet.

Touching me and thinking about a gun
at the same time. Thinking about a gun
because he's touching me.
An answer for Jessper.

He felt a storm—I felt that
in the weight of his hand pressing on my knee
as if it were a melon, to extract a sweeter liquid
than tears so much easier to extract
from this life.

Rain
in the air, the flight trail of hawks, turkey
buzzards, the small
rain

of mulberries falling from teeth.

squirrels and bats making their way between treetops,
stirring up pine into the soup that was air

the soup about to boil.

(Dob found out that John Parker,
a black man, owned a foundry in Ohio.
Dob found out from a traveling man
that black men could make guns.
He'd hire himself out to get the money.
Didn't want to steal one of Master Perry's.
Wants to buy his own.
What happened to Esmenda's guns?
Had Dwarf Sully opened the barrels
with his bare hands and bent them into our spoons?)

Lightning in the distance.
Cotton field briefly lighting up.

Arms around me. My head against his chest.
The smell of his work.

"If these arms were guns,
they could hold you better,"

Dob said
then he was quiet
so we could kiss

so daybreak could come.

ALONE WITH RALLS JANET

Me and Ralls Janet scrub laundry in the river,
two young women and not a bit of trust.
Silent as the turtles. Scrubbing together.
Bedding atop the river like a layer of rippling ice.

Exhausting.
Bedding triples its weight holding water.
Squeezed out in stages. Takes the two of us.
That wrestling almost fulfills a dream of sails
going where I direct them.
Didn't want to boil garments today, fire around the bottom
of the washtub as if the tub sits on a flaming leaf.
Didn't want heat. No burning. Cold wash. Despite the inconvenience.
To be nearer trees reaching over the river with their branches,
as if to scoop it up, put out fire, soothing smell of last fruit
uneaten, unpicked, becoming on the limb wine
which won't be salvaged,
shriveling like my hands in this water tumbling over them,
cooling them, few knuckles peeled back like seed pods,
fingers starting to look as if they're wearing rags
where soap the hands made tears up again
the skin that cotton burs tore up first.
It looks as if something's been eating me.
I can use my knuckles as thimbles.

Soap atop the river like clusters of eggs. Frogs
and striders to come. Soap like trains of fragile
carriages. Hands aching in the cold. Want
to feel this. Wish it were colder. Plenty of good basket grass.
Jessper's so good at weaving baskets you want them to be hats.
As good with hair. Used to do Eveline Staley's hair
so beautifully, even though Eveline could barely lift her head,
until the burn. Jessper.

Got here early, deer drinking,
very little sign of the power of the sun.
Some clouds. Small things drinking dew.
Shaking out the bedding, catching a cloud falling.

Castle Soap Ralls Janet bought
to release dirt and Ralls Janet
enjoying that release. The most animated
she's ever looked. How excited
she is to make that dirt get out.
She is exhilarated by the exile.
She has a cake of *Castle*
dwindling.

Her problems, all of which are black like dirt,
floating away.

Her husband and her daughter in Kentucky.
Dwarf Sully there to groom and jockey.
Pearl off midwifing;
couldn't get back in time to go with him for luck.
It's Jessper. Mamalee helping.
I didn't want to be there.
She should have run when I told her to.
Poison couldn't stop this.
Poison caused it. Cold, cold scrubbing.

Dob?

Ralls Janet sighs. We can share that
exasperation. We can't share her husband
whom I don't want. Who loves me
maybe even more intensely. I rub my thimbles
as cake of *Castle* continues to dwindle.

Dob is better
in every way for me.
Won't tell her that
he has to be.

Easier time of year. After harvest.
Putting up more fruit and vegetables later.
Not now. Cake of *Castle* continues to dwindle.
Her taste for plums has become disgust,
so many of them perfect. Plum bread
and gravy. Mamalee has plummed everything
Ralls Janet eats and needs. Feels like an intruder
which she is
in Mamalee's plum home.

Again she sighs.

"You want to say something?" I ask her.
Her lips part, then she hesitates.

"Can't anybody hear you but some animals.
Go on and speak if you want to. I won't hurt you, Ralls Janet."

She looks stunned by that, not comforted;
stares at me.

All my things are clean in a basket,
unbuttoned cocoon on the bottom—I don't feel right
without it on, I've gotten so used to it. So comfortable
in my bold protection.

"You better hurry; I'm about to hang these
up to dry. Then I've got other things to do."

"Varl. . . . " she said softly. Said that way,
there wasn't a better word for truce.

"Varl. . . . I think about leaving."

I couldn't believe that she had said that.
What was she trying to get at? Why was she talking to me
like this, as if for comfort, advice; as if for friendship, a combining
of forces—two young women of predicament? For help?
I didn't trust it. Why all of a sudden?

"Why do that? You have everything, Miss Perry."

"Please don't mock me."

"I wasn't mocking you. You *do* have everything.
Good-looking prospering husband. Beautiful child.
The wealth of the south in your land and
only rare valuable slaves. Growing diversity
of businesses. The winning horses.
Your own pretty face and incomparable color.
That's enough of everything.
Go further
and you'd have to take on contradiction
which would just wreck what's already
performing adequately on the list.
It may not be possible to get more than what you have.
A maximum existence might be yours."

"I want to read more than my husband's mind.
Really. It's not helping me to feed on resentment
all day long. You just get smarter and smarter
and more appealing to him. I don't like it."

"Ralls Janet, I wouldn't—"

"—Yes, you would, Varl.
You've been belittling me all along.
You'd let him do anything to you

just to keep it from me.
But that's not getting you anything either.
Just as wasted as my resentment.
I'm tired of this, Varl.
What are you accomplishing?
I'm not the one enslaving you.
I'm not the one who can free you."

"Neither is he."

She looked stunned. Couldn't find a response
right away.
Couldn't bring herself to stare
right away.

A bit too defiant for her. Not settling into
the overture of camaraderie. Soap had cleared
that space on the surface of the water,
but I'd already filled it with a deep-current grudge.
Couldn't just overlook it.

"You started *this*, Ralls Janet. *This* coming clean, *this* confession
for the sake of setting up a truce, and *this* animosity still fresh
between us. You resented me from the moment you got here.
Banished me from sleeping in the house to sleeping in a cabin
you made your husband build practically before
you would walk through the door of the house.
You didn't know anything about me. It could have been
different, but you let me know you were my inferior
from the beginning. At that point I'd done nothing
for you or against you. Maybe I could've been loyal
to something other than your assumptions."

She'd waited too long to try to reach me;
she'd let me get too far away and away with too much.
I didn't need anything from her, and she knew it.

To pull her out, I'd have to get sucked back in
deeper than I'd been in the first place.
I hadn't tried on subservience
and didn't know how she'd take it off.
It wasn't just a matter of reading.
Subservience fit her. It was her size.
She really was Ralls Janet.
There was no need for an experiment.

"I'll just hang my things on these branches
so you can take your time
if you're not finished speaking."

"Your mother isn't trouble. Just you, Varl.
I've talked to her before. While you're on that tree stump
with Dob and my husband.
I've talked to her. In the woods
she's tried to convince my husband to treat me better.
It's you. Too much has happened since I married Peter
for you to still base everything on what
I did in haste, in error, and out of fear. You've seen
too much and you've caused too much to keep holding
the circumstances of my arrival against me.
Mamalee doesn't hold that against me. She's helping me.
I can read your name now. It's on too many of his papers.
Varl, Varl, Varl. You and that magnificent
dead horse. Nothing else has a chance with him.
And you help to keep it that way. You go out of your way
to maintain your status with him. Why?
You don't have to go beyond being his slave.
Nothing further is required, so why do you go so far?"

"Why do you assume that *slave* must mean
just one simple thing? Maybe *slave* is much bigger
than you can imagine. Maybe your husband can see that
even if he can't understand it. A slave is what I am,

maybe all that I am. Despite how we're talking
a slave is what I am. We wouldn't have to have this talk
if I wasn't a slave. If I were free, I wouldn't associate
with you at all."

"You are not what comes to mind when I think of slaves."

"I'm what comes to my mind when I think of slaves.
When Peter Perry thinks of slaves. Nobody but you
seems to have elevated me to something above slave.
I'm a slave to him, nothing but a slave. But can't a slave
have feelings? Can't a slave be the object
of somebody's feelings? Whatever his feelings are for me,
aren't they his feelings for his slave?
His feelings for you are his feelings for his wife.
Those can't be the same feelings because *slave*
and *wife* aren't the same. They might be close,
but not the same."

"He's confused and troubled sorting out
what he wants and doesn't want,
what he can have and can't.
It's sickness.
Nothing adds up like it's supposed to.
Some rules can't be broken, some can
but if they can, then they weren't rules.
He wants to know the rules."

"You want me to explain them to him?"

"Give him permission not to care about you.
Give him permission not to be your master."

"He already has that, Ralls Janet.
There is no rule that he has to be my master
or anybody's master. Plenty of men aren't masters.

He's getting something out of it that he wants.
He doesn't want me so much that he can't see
anything else. You're making me too important
to him. Forget about trying to capture
his attention, and just work on paying attention
to yourself. I'm not his life. I'm not even with him.
He's more than a hundred miles away.
Ralls Janet, I don't know what to do for you,
not that I want to do anything for you."

"Leave, Varl. I order you to run away."

"What?"

She just stole from me what I was saving
for my finale. She stole it.
If I leave, I'll be obeying Ralls Janet.
She'll be my mistress if I leave.

I sigh. I can't believe it.
Varl defeated.

She repeats it, on her feet, gesturing
with gloved fingers. "I order you to run away.
RUN AWAY!" Almost pleading.

Her back to me, Ralls Janet trembling,
but surprising me further, not sinking to the ground.
Queen of the dwindled *Castle*.

Nothing left to hang
but pages of cocoon. I don't want her
to see them even though she can't read
anything in them but *Varl*.
Not meant for her. Hang them. Expose them.

She stole from *me*.

"It's all right, Varl. You're still a slave
even if you don't act like one
I'm still the mistress
even ... Words don't always mean something.
They don't. That's why I don't have to ask you
if you love him."

She grabbed some cocoon pages from the branches
over which they were draped like odd white fruit.
"It's not the words," she whispered to herself.

I also grabbed some pages and threw them at her.

"Go ahead, Ralls Janet. Keep them. Rip them.
Burn them. Go ahead. Burning doesn't always
destroy something. Go ahead.
The pages still happened.
I still thought the thoughts,
felt the feelings. Go ahead.
Burn down *our master's* entire library. Go ahead."

She gathered them and handled them like heirloom lace.
Neatly folded and stacked them. Looked beyond me.

"We had an orchard with a thousand trees
when I was a girl, Varl. In the spring
thousands and thousands of barely pink and pinker
flowers. And the bees and butterflies that would come
finding thousands of wells in the flowers. How deep
those wells must have been to those insects.
How precious to the hummingbirds. But nothing like this.
Nothing like this." Stack of my sacred pages
on her palm
which was another page.

VARL AND THE STAR-SHOULDERED DRESS

Mamalee wakes me
with a hunk of bread all moist with buttermilk
dropped on my forehead that she says is hot enough
to fry the bread
because I've stayed asleep so long
with the sun shining through a crack in the cabin wall
and aiming straight
for my head.

I have never slept so long.
Maybe the master has just been murdered.
There are more and more whisperings of rebellion.

More and more interest in guns.
This has gone on too long.

The buttermilk's thick and sticky.
Drops of it
run down my face slowly,
like candles melting into light.

Mamalee hands me a rag to wipe my face.

We keep a stunning little garden
and Pearl goes after plants from the deep woods.
Okra, checkerberry, blue elder embedded in the bread.

 "What's happened?"

"It's late, isn't it? You noticed.
Well, we're celebrating the renaming of *Perrysburg;*
it's *Varlton* now; we live in *Varlton,* Tennessee.

And we're devastated by or perhaps celebrating
some scandal. Apparently
there's something on Little Miss Lusa
that won't come off. And she says you did it.
Ralls Janet was over here sneaking me—because of you—
out before dawn, saying she didn't really want *you*
at the house today. Didn't want to have to look
at *you*. You're fortunate that Peter Perry
is a peculiar man; he seems to be a bit amused
by what happened to his daughter shortly after
Perrysburg became *Varlton*.
But Varl, something like this
when you should try to be a woman of discretion—"

"—Something like what?"

"Please, Girl; you did it, so you know."

"*Lusa* can't lie? *Ralls Janet* can't scheme?"

"No; Ralls Janet definitely can't scheme
without somebody helping her."

"Who would help her, Mamalee, but you?
You're confused; you had so much loyalty
for Esmenda Dube that you haven't exhausted it yet
and it's spilling over onto Ralls Janet
who doesn't deserve it. Ordering me to run away!"

"Well, you can't say that you weren't warned
not to take so many disrespectful liberties with her.
Maybe you went too far in the open. Got that man
to name his town after you—*out in the open*. Says
it's to honor his horse that's been dead almost
eighteen years. It's named for *you*. This is dangerous.
I have to think about the system of the traveling men.

That must be protected. And it's getting harder
in the midst of these uprisings that slaveholders
are finding more difficult to suppress. Instigators
coming in to ignite insurrection. Traveling men
trying to stick to quiet caution—you are too much of a risk
to be involved. Leader of a personal rebellion. *Varlton.*

Ralls Janet's not as weak as you think.
You've been goading her meekness for years. In fact,
you are Peter Perry's accomplice; you assist him
in goading her. And this has got to be
her limit. *Varlton.*

What have you permitted with that man? He promised
me—but I didn't realize that I should have made *you*
promise, too. You go too far. Too much empowerment.
But we'll talk about that later.

Apparently, Lusa has had some involvement with indigo
reminiscent of that mud incident you sponsored a while back.
Everybody suspected you even before Lusa
told her mother what you had done to her
trying to make her your sister. Or worse,
what Ralls Janet believes: Trying to steal that child
from pitiful Ralls Janet and turn her into something
you could have had with Master Peter."

"Involvement with indigo?
Does this really sound like something
I would need to do? Me?"

"If that was the only way you could have Dob
and keep Master Peter—get used to saying that again as if you
mean it: *Master* Peter—distant and cold to *Mistress* Ralls Janet,
you'd do it. I wonder if you know just how much
of your love for Dob might just be spite against your master?

Would you love him if you were free to love
anybody you wanted?"

"I already have Dob and I'm quite secure about
that having. I'm not going to question any Dob thing."

"Your attitude is a mistake.
Well, whether you did it or not, you've been blamed."

"Little *Spotted* Lusa is going to make her father much richer.
He'll get her anything she wants. No wonder we got
the day off."

"Varl, this is serious," Mamalee says, "but he did invite
his Aunt Baly-Belinda Rouper to inaugurate the Bank of Varlton.
As for his wife, she wants revenge. Ralls Janet brought over
this dress. You're to wear it." She hands it to me.
"Oh, it's not one of hers; it's one of Lusa's.
You're not to ever wear any other dress again."

I throw it down. The nerve
of Ralls Janet.

Why did he do it? Extreme deviancy? To rename his town,
to honor me—I'd like to talk with him as Ralls Janet
did with me, but I don't dare. Why should I need a more powerful
message than a white man naming his town after
his young slavegirl he has loved? The love cannot get bigger
than something he can fit his whole town into; people
who don't love me yet live in Varlton are encompassed.
He's named his privilege *Varlton. Varlton* is the name
of his success. But why? To make me more his

or to make me too big to own, so big I take on a life
of my own after he planted a seed? Named so he can live
more comfortably inside what I represent to him, a way

not to lose that? To show me what he's willing to risk
because he really loves me? To make it geographical fact?

Too powerful a message to be just injury on a wife so easy
to injure. Too big for that. So much to think about.

Is this a kindness? To have a Varlton, you must first
have a slave—is this a kindness? Varl of Varlton.
No—fact is, to have a Varlton, you must first have
that horse. You must have doubt. How much has the master
changed? Are you always held captive by the roots?

Mamalee sits and unplaits her hair. It was
sort of a copper color, a sun gift. Not
as coppery as Captain's, which was a birth gift.
The sun was turning Mamalee's hair
the color of Master Peter's ax handles.
It was thick enough to hide a gun in it.
Two guns.

It was pretty long, too;
if all those tight curls were stretched out all
the way, it would look as if she had vines
growing out of her head, as if from her head
squash and pumpkins could be harvested.
As if her ideas were bursting with seeds.
Soft around her face, as if her face was dressed up
in her hair and she was going someplace she'd
never been before so had to look fancier
than she'd ever looked before, but she plaited
her hair back small, but even as small
as she could make it, it could still hide something.
She could still pull a surprise out of it

if she had to, if
she needed to ruin Master Peter's surprise
of any minute coming close up on what's his
to claim it. Though she suspected he already had,
perhaps by invitation.

Talking as she braids. Her fingers part of the vine
coming alive with the movement.
"I worked on the dress some while you were sleep.
It's pretty small. I did what I could, but you've
got to wear it. She said to tell you that *her husband*
—she emphasized *her husband* just like that—said
that she could order you to wear it seeing as
it's *Varlton* Day."

I tried to deflect the stinging.

"Mamalee, maybe Lusa was just playing
with pokeberries or taking a bath in plum skins
left to ferment. I doubt she actually had any
involvement with indigo.

I remember playing with pokeberries and making
superficial dye years ago; I rubbed the berries
on my fingernails and nothing happened that lasted,
just a little color for a little while. Got lighter and
lighter when I scrubbed Lusa's clothes.

But my mouth held on the longest. As if from then on
my words needed to come out of purple doors.
As if purple lips would make me say grander things,
as if saying grander things would let grander thoughts
take over my head and turn my mind purple, as if
saying grander things would make grander things happen.
I still have interest in grander things, and it's building;
the interest is building itself to grander dimensions

of which Dob is a big part.
When it faded from my lips, I told Jessper that Dob
had kissed it off until it was gone."

"Did Dob know you were about such saying back then?"

"I hope so. That's why I said it.
Jessper believed me. She was like Lusa Perry is now
in that. Believes all of what I say, as if
I can't invent a lie."

"You believe that?"

"Why would *Master* Perry allow this? He *told* her
she could force this dress on me? He's a *partner*
to this? Why? He stopped doing what she wanted
a long time ago unless it just happened to coincide
with what he wanted. And I know he doesn't want this
for me. Not something humiliating like this."

"Apparently he *does*, Varl. He supports this.
Probably to keep the spark of Mistress Ralls Janet's
newfound gumption from going out. Wants to see
what it might do with the opportunity to do something.
Makes her more interesting to him; what she should
have done long ago: arrange confrontations with you
if he was that important to her. But I suspect really
he might be looking much further ahead.
To what comes after this. Your response. What
she does next in this war. And, Varl, you are a slave;
he is humiliating you all the time he owns you.
He doesn't love you if he keeps you his slave.
For your own good, remember you are a slave."

"He could love me. He could keep me a slave to keep me
any way at all, for fear if free I wouldn't have him, but as my

master, I have to call him mine; even if brutally
we are linked. And now linked tighter in
the Battle of Varlton. To be fought to a decisive finish
culminating in surrender. It's my move."

Day ages.

Lusa's old dress, redone a bit,
let out as much as it could be.
Mamalee had made it leaving plenty
of letting-out room in it,
had I gotten it a year or two sooner
not quite enough now,
and she embroidered stars
about the shoulders because she remembered
how much I liked stars back then when she made it,
and now the star-shouldered dress is mine,
the cloth of it still crisp around the hem,
whether or not it fits.

A beautiful dress it is
for a smaller girl. This is from Ralls Janet.
Lusa has nothing to do with this.
From Ralls Janet who knows
I have not well resisted an envelope of cloth,
my cocoon around me, like a mama to me,
all the hot nights, all the cold.
But this is insult and revenge.
A diminishing.
To get the small tight thing on, my cocoon
must come off. To wear the small tight thing
everyday, my cocoon must stay off
before the moth is fully converted.
I can't trust this dress.
Not the dress I was wearing
when Master Peter came close up on me.

Just *this* dress.
I'm wearing a dress all the time.
I sleep in a dress.
Wash one dress while I'm wearing the other.
Work in a dress. Think, dream, and write in a dress.
Fall in love with Dob in a dress.
But not this dress.

I used to want this one,
lacy inlays, buttons of antler and bone,
a dress of such a flowing range
of color, it could take the place of spring.

I wanted to dress up in meaning, to have on something
that couldn't make a mistake, that wouldn't be
misunderstood, even when it was limp, and hanging from
a rope, the wind poking at it all day long. I wanted that.
There's nothing wrong with having wanted that.

Now it's mine. I have to put it on
distorted.

I have to get by with recollection
of magnificence, past glory, and purpose.
I am not meant to have ambition.

Ralls Janet surprised me. I didn't think
she could devise anything so dastardly perfect;
Lusa's dress fits a child because a child is what Lusa is.
Their only child. The one and only master baby.

Ralls Janet said she wasn't having more children,
said she couldn't give life to anything else.
It was a good thing, she said, that Lusa was perfect.
Perfection finishes you. And I am finished
with the perfect dress.

I put on the redone, let-out, star-shouldered dress
knowing I'll be hearing from the master baby
when she sees me in it, a little peeved to see that
it's me who brought the stars out in it, and not her.
Seeing the stars, she'll demand it back, but

when I give it back, because I'm not keeping it,
there won't be any more stars, and I'll be sure
to return it on a starless evening. Then
I'll open my hand and show her a pile of stars
that I've pulled down, and I'll make her promise
me something that if she'll do it, I'll put the stars back
just so she won't be without wishes

and the ones of her wishes that appeal to my power
will be the ones that might happen; *you can never tell
anybody about that or you can never be sure what I might
do*, I'll say to Lusa, *to you*. Then I'll disappear

just as for a moment I disappear in the dress till it
slides as far as it can down my body and my head
pokes through the opening. Seams rather strained.
And then I realize, right then, corner of a star
in my mouth, that it won't succeed
in belittling me as Ralls Janet hoped.
The dress is small,
not me. In it, I seem even bigger.
I might break the seams and burst right out of it
if I exert myself, if I reach out to shake her hand
in gratitude. I might burst out of
a star-shouldered cocoon while Peter is looking
and is glad that he has eyes.

Oh yes.
Even if I obey Ralls Janet and run,
Peter Perry might run after me.

Obey her
and she might still be in Varlton. Buried
alive in Varlton.
What did it matter?

So much to think about
And thinking is its own important thing.
How to handle your situation. How to attack. Defend.
How to become free. A cocoon has been the most useful
thing for thinking. Maybe the only privacy. Inside it, thinking has
been the main Varl thing. Being slave
has been secondary, only on the outside.
Changing inside it
to what I've thought of. Thinking
about changing my life. Every time
I think and every time I write, I'm changing my life.
Changing what happened, changing what can happen
because a changed Varl has options
for the geography of that dress made in Varlton

that are different from the options of a Varl
who could not write this.

A DAY IN VARLTON

Activity in the cocoons
Dob and I found in the woods
in Varlton.

Near a holding cave
for guns Dob's been off collecting
for a planned insurrection. Soon.
King of this.

He finally told me.

I held my breath and watched
something becoming free
in Varlton,

an inconsequential insect
whose purpose was for me,
beauty and integrity, becoming free
however briefly.

Such power.
Cocoon splitting
in Varlton.

Water in the cup rippled
more than my walking had been rippling it,
more than the effects of kissing Dob.

I kiss Dob
not Master Peter

in the Varlton
he made for me.

He loved making Varlton. Place to live out challenging days.
Place to challenge days. With or without a map I know how
to find Varlton.

Breeze rippled, picked up sass and speed

Corn swayed

Clouds and nighttime danced out of the way
and freed the sun

Ralls Janet moved out the way of the window
so that sun could be free, too, to get in deeper
in the room. Like a dagger. In Varlton.

Varlton splitting.

Cocoon splitting wider.

"You're Free," I said to the luna moth.
" You're free," Dob said to the other.

Sully stopped feeding the horses.

Pearl ignored the chickens.

Peter Perry noticed
and complimented the strangeness.
Marveled at what it had accomplished
—perhaps his ways had helped—

though there was less of it, rebellions
against propriety
becoming practically routine.

Extending beyond
the boundaries of Varlton.

Mules stopped.
Flies stopped droning.
Birds stopped but the air held them.
Hearts stopped. Life stopped for a moment

most of everything was freed for a moment

though the luna moths didn't have time to stop

their flight out of Varlton
through the split in time.

Their wings magnificent green pages
in a book come true.

No matter where they go
coming back to Varlton will be coming home.
That name particularly welcoming.

—I'll follow Dob sometimes
and sometimes he'll follow me.